Prime Markets in Canada

Consumer Demand Prediction and Broadly Based Selection of Market Location

Garbis Armen, BA, MRTPI, PhD

iUniverse, Inc.
Bloomington

Prime Markets in Canada
Consumer Demand Prediction and Broadly Based Selection of Market Location

iUniverse books may be ordered through booksellers or by contacting:

iUniverse
1663 Liberty Drive
Bloomington, IN 47403
www.iuniverse.com
1-800-Authors (1-800-288-4677)

ISBN: 978-1-4620-0368-6 (sc)
ISBN: 978-1-4620-0370-9 (ebk)

Printed in the United States of America

iUniverse rev. date: 06/07/2011

ACKNOWLEDGMENTS

I am grateful to Prof. Sir Peter Hall for his supervision of my PhD thesis and to Dr Ronald Ng, School of Oriental & African Studies, Un of London, UK.

CONTENTS

APPENDICES

Diagrams

Tables

INTRODUCTION

When your family looks for a new house in a town, every member will ask about the location of facilities related to his or her daily, weekly, monthly or other needs - going to school, play area, doctor's surgery, grocer, hairdresser, post office, bus stop, etc. This is a broadly-based location selection, considering personal needs first and connections second - length of walks, car and bike journeys, bus stop location - all meant to ensure convenience for every family member. The same approach, spread over the scale of the second largest country of the world, will be used here to help inventors and entrepreneurs select the best market for their specific new product, service, or innovative facility, to improve the standard of living of the great variety of ethnicities and persons living in Canada. This book will also be of interest to various government tiers, local and foreign investors as well as citizens, intent to enjoy all that this beautiful country and smart inventors can offer, to improve the quality of life for residents and visitors alike.

Back in 1905, when Prime Minister Sir Wilfred Laurier told his people that "The 20th century will be Canada's century", he probably meant that while in the 19th century the country's resources had been just extracted and exported with little gain, "in the 20th we shall also manufacture and sell goods to earn more". As the century wore on however, advancing technology made services far more important than manufacturing and the majority of Canadians found themselves employed in service and construction, rather than manufacturing industries. Moreover, they soon embraced also a strange industry called briefly IT – Information Technology - to the extent that every newborn Canadian, by the age of 4 can ask and get a toy computer to play with and by his or her teens, buy an i-phone or "blackberry" to chatter with boyfriends or gossip endlessly with girl friends.

Services and IT will continue to grow, providing not only our 'daily bread' but also our joys and quality of life. Businessmen in Canada and abroad will find here how and where to make the best of opportunities arising from the provision of these joys and services in this country. The busy CEO with little time to spare, by looking up the diagrams and maps, will grasp the approach and turn to the Appendices to select the city regions offering him the best sites to locate his outlets for highest profit. Town Hall professionals too, will find out how to take into account the social and economic characteristics of each neighbourhood in their town and locate facilities to be of maximum use to the community. Quality development for housing, shops, novel services, institutions and even statues and monuments, could all be tuned to emphasize local character and create a 'sense of place' - a feeling that the scenes, sounds and even smells experienced in an area are all tuned to the performance of a function. Towns built on a natural feature - a mountain or a beach - added to an event promoted by a smart initiator of celebration, the fame of a whole town

Garbis Armen, BA, MRTPI, PhD

may be built - like Chamonix or Champagne, Seville or Sheffield. Green forests and plentiful snow, added to Canada's many victories in the 2010 Winter Olympic Games, could be the start for Whistler to develop in that direction and become a town with a 'sense of place'.

POTENTIAL CONSUMER POPULATION

Each demographic division of the population which you hope to attract to buy your innovative product or service, has a certain probability to buy it. Adding up all demographic divisions, each multiplied by its probability, will give the total Potential Consumer Population for your product

SLIMMING COURSE Age characteristics	LADIES' TOOLS Socio-Economic characteristics	MUTUAL FUND Income characteristics	ENGLISH NOVEL Language characteristics
Ages 0 - 19	Managers/ Professionals	$10k - 29.9k	Anglophone
Swingers	Clerical work'rs	$30k - 49.9k	Francophone
Parents	Skilled work'rs	$50k - 79.9k	Chinese
Retired	All other work'rs	$80k +	Allophone

Proportion of TOTAL POPULATION OF A REGION
Uninterested in your product or service

Proportion of Total, with a Probability to buy Your Service is the
TOTAL CONSUMER POPULATION You can count upon

DIAG. 01: Only the people with the RELEVANT CHARACTERISTICS have a PROBABILITY to buy your innovative product or service. Add all the demographic groups which have such a probability and You will find the total POTENTIAL CONSUMER POPULATION FOR YOUR PRODUCT - **YOUR PRIME MARKET IN CANADA.**

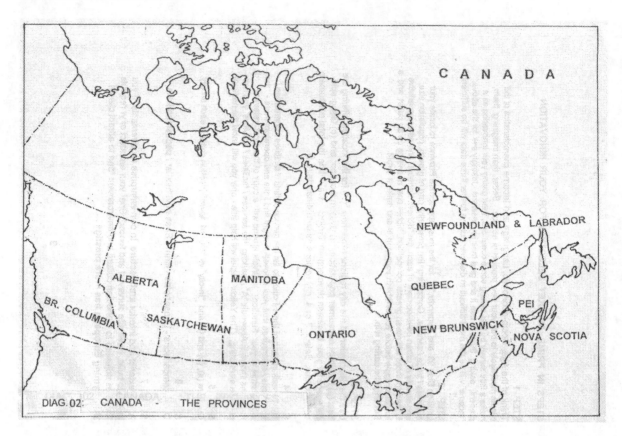

DIAG. 02:   CANADA -   THE PROVINCES

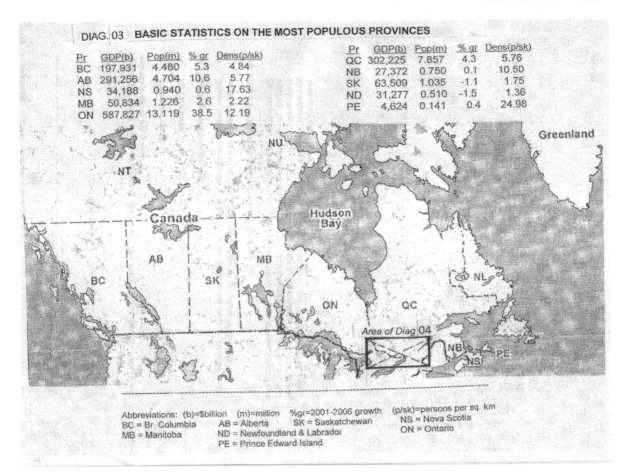

DIAG. 03   BASIC STATISTICS ON THE MOST POPULOUS PROVINCES

Pr	GDP(b)	Pop(m)	% gr	Dens(p/sk)
BC	197,931	4.480	5.3	4.84
AB	291,256	4.704	10.6	5.77
NS	34,188	0.940	0.6	17.63
MB	50,834	1.226	2.6	2.22
ON	587,827	13.119	38.5	12.19

Pr	GDP(b)	Pop(m)	% gr	Dens(p/sk)
QC	302,225	7.857	4.3	5.76
NB	27,372	0.750	0.1	10.50
SK	63,509	1.035	-1.1	1.75
ND	31,277	0.510	-1.5	1.36
PE	4,624	0.141	0.4	24.98

Abbreviations: (b)=$billion   (m)=million   %gr=2001-2006 growth   (p/sk)=persons per sq. km
BC = Br. Columbia   AB = Alberta   SK = Saskatchewan   NS = Nova Scotia
MB = Manitoba   ND = Newfoundland & Labrador   ON = Ontario
                       PE = Prince Edward Island

1. CANADA AS A MARKERTING ENVIRONMENT

The mounting prosperity, safe banking system, minimal crime rate, venture some approach to business and lively spirit of Canadians, makes this country and people an attractive environment to establish just about any innovative product or service required by the growing population. Let's consider some of these market qualities one by one, on the basis of 2010 statistics compiled by *"The Economist"* –

- The GDP was $1,428 billion in 2009 while it was barely $297 billion in 1968 when the GDP concept was established and by 2005 amounted to $1024.9 billion. Canada is the 10th largest exporter of products with 2.62% of the total World exports emanating from this country;

- The *'economic freedom index'** amounted to 80.0 while for Sweden it was only 70.5; for UK it was 79.0; and only USA's was slightly higher at 80.7;

- The *'1997-2008 house-price indicators'* table had Canada at 12th place –Equal to USA - with a 66% increase, compared to South Africa in the 1st place with 389% and UK at 6th place with 150% increase;

- The *"Largest population in 2007"* table indicated Canada (32.9 million) as 36th, compared with USA (303.9m) at 3rd place and UK (60.0m) at 22nd place;

- The *"2009 population aged over 60"* table had Canada at 32nd place with 19.5% compared with Japan at 1st place with 29.7%, and UK at 16th place with 22.4%;

- The *"Average annual population growth for 2010-2015"* will amount to 0.92**%;**

- The *"urban population in 2006"* was 80.3%, while in 1986 it was only 76 %; This 80.3% of Canada's population - accessible through the various markets shown in Appendices B and C - live in 13 large Metro Areas (accommodating nearly 18 million people); 100 cities over 45,000 population each (some 21 million people); and no fewer than 230 towns of more than 15,000 people each.

Most of these urban areas are part of the three Concepts of Growth in Canada, as shown on Diag. 04 –

1

A) The ***"Golden Horseshoe"***, the most prosperous and most rapidly growing area of Canada, within easy reach of USA, comprising some 8.1 million people in 2006 and grown to 9.0m in 2010;

B) The ***"Golden Crescent"***, in which three of the six largest Canadian Metro Conurbations are located, comprising some 13.6 million people; Third is -

C) The ***"Windsor to Quebec"*** growth axis containing both Golden Horseshoe and Crescent and comprising some 14.7million people.

Canada's area of some 10 million square kms (second only to Russia) may be mostly uninhabitable at present, but with advancing global warming, reinforced plastics technology and transparent geodesic domes covering markets and even small towns, will make it quite possible to accommodate several millions more people by 2020.

Canada's policy of multiculturalism has reinforced the "open doors" immigration policy dating back to the 1880's. This policy will be adopted by most countries wishing to see their economy grow. Canada had the highest immigration in the world (240,000 – 265,000 annum) and immigrants are often innovative, adventurous and cross the oceans with private enterprise in mind. The first people to benefit from this liberal immigration policy were 46,000 Empire Loyalists (from the original 13 United States) who entered in 1755-1815 and with their private enterprise initiative established thriving services and manufactures in Ontario, Quebec and the Atlantic provinces.

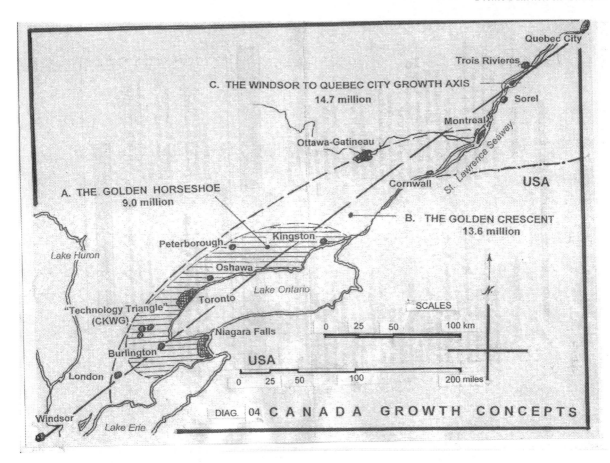

DIAG. 04 C A N A D A   G R O W T H   C O N C E P T S

Canadians today are grateful to the First Nations for their cabin and canoe-building skills, treaty land donations, as well as cultural traditions; To the French and English Founding Nations whose languages are now official and serve as the means of communication with the rest of the world; And finally to millions of Europeans who came to toil on the Provinces and the grain industry, in addition to building cities and villages by the hundred. Thus, the 600 self-governing bands of the First Nations and the 10 Provinces where most of the Founding Nation and European peoples live and develop today, form the Canadian Nation, in the approximate proportions shown below:-

TABLE 1 . ETHNIC ORIGINS OF THE CANADIAN POPULATION, AS STATED IN CENSUS 2001

.. responded just:"Canadian" 32.2%			Predominant in Province	
... responded just:"Quebecois" 66.2%				
	English	21.0	NL	97.7
	French	18.9	NB	32.6
	Scottish	15.1	NS	29.3
	Irish	13.9	NS	19.9
	German	10.2	SK	30.0
	Italian	4.6	ON	7.0
	Chinese	4.3	BC	10.6
	NA Indian	4.1	Nun	83.6
	Ukrainian	3.9	AB	10.2
	Dutch	3.3	BC	5.3
	E. Indian	3.1	BC	6.4
	Russian	1.6	SK	4.2
	Metis	1.3	MB	6.4

Each of these 15 ethnic groups may be assumed to exercise a different taste for food, goods and other preferences. If the Entrepreneur requires the composition of a particular region or neighbourhood in detail, he may find it in the Statistics Canada website shown in the References. In the broad-based approach to market selection here, all the above are divided into four broadly representative consumer groupings :-

Anglophone, Francophone, Oriental and Allophone .

In a "Census Snapshot of Canada – URBANIZATION" pamphlet dated March 2009, Statistics Canada stated that the country's population was becoming increasingly urbanized:- from 76% in 1986; to 78% in 1996 and 80.3% in 2006; Total population growth from 1956 to 1981 was 9% in each 5-yr inter-censal period; It was 4% between 1996 and 2001 and 5.4% between 2001 and 2006; As of 2006 no less than 68% of Canadians lived in a CMA, while 45% lived in one of the six largest CMAs – i.e. Toronto, Montreal, Vancouver, Ottawa-Gatineau, Calgary or Edmonton - all of which accounted for 66% of Canada's 2001-2006 growth.

Toronto is Canada's economic capital and one of the top financial centres of the world. Representing multicultural Canada (49% of her population born abroad) she** continues to receive most of the immigrants. She is the 5th largest megalopolis on the American continent and has a great future as a world mega-city. It is already a Global City by virtue of her** major functions: Finance, Telecoms, Arts, Aerospace, Media, Film, TV, Publishing, Software, Medicine, Research, Tourism and Education.

NOTE: * "**Economic** Freedom Index"= Created in 1995 by the Heritage Foundation and the Wall Street Journal, it is based on Adam Smith's "The Wealth of Nations". It amounts to "*Absolute right of ownership; Freedom to move labour, capital and goods; Absence of coercion;and Liberty beyond the citizen's expectation to "protect and maintain liberty itself*". It covers property rights, Business, Trade, Investment, Labour, Government size, Fiscal, Financial, Monetary freedoms and absence of Corruption".

NOTE: ** The CITY being referred to as a female ("Toronto and HER major functions", as written above) is the style to be followed, because the Greek "POLIS" and the French "VILLE" are feminine and "SHE" is therefore duly respectful.

2. MARKETING YOUR INNOVATION

This and the subsequent two Sections will deal with three paramount factors for the successful establishment of outlets to market your innovation -

A. The distribution of the most likely consumers for your product, service or facility; This is CONSUMER SPACE;

B. The distribution of services, social facilities and institutions existing in the city region, with which your service or social activity will establish linkages – exchange of products, raw materials, as well as prestige; This is SYSTEM LOCATION SPACE;

C. The distribution of geographical factors – proximity to a beach, mountains, favourable features, climate conditions, or generators of pollution; This is GEOGRAPHICAL SPACE.

THE DISTRIBUTION OF CONSUMERS

Whatever service or product you invent, will spread by word of mouth or as news broadcast on TV, or by being seen in use by neighbours and gratefully - or secretly - copied or plagiarized. If the invention works, they will tell their friends and they will tell their friends and so on. This is shown as a solid on Diag. 08, except that:-

(a) The information from person-to-person is transmitted by Monte Carlo chance; and

(b) The scale of the bell-curve is country-wide, rather than city- or market-wide.

Capitals of kingdoms were centrally located for optimal defence and to spread the king's proclamations quickly. As roads were improved however, coaches ran faster, motor cars took over, electrical wires and electronic chips transmitted messages in seconds. Winnipeg in the middle of Canada is the ideal centre for the rapid diffusion of heavy product inventions.

Today, news of innovations are transmitted by TV – the fastest social medium available today. The distribution of service outlets however, still has to accord with the residential location of the most relevant consumers, because visual inspection, testing, or sample trial tasting, are still important for non-standardized goods, to ensure quality.

The development and diffusion of a novel activity or product - from person-to-person and country to country - has been repeated from times immemorial. The most important recent additions have been *"patenting"* to protect the inventor; Setting up standards and safe use procedures by the state; Development of less expensive variations of an invention by competitors; Sophistication and streamlining of marketing - including fast vacuum-drawn packaging - to minimize the waste of time.

Marketing an innovation, as the main subject of the concept to be put forward, is to be discussed from an invention's birth to its diffusion over a region, by planting it at the right place for fast maximum spread and profit. The 'right place' is where first and foremost, the people of the most relevant age, socio-economic structure, disposable income, culture and technical know-how, live in a region or area. Once these people purchase, use, taste and talk about the innovation to friends, colleagues, acquaintances and strangers, the seed has been successfully planted. This is diffusion *par excellence*.

A pioneering study on the subject was published by Swedish professor, Torsten Hägerstrand in 1953 under a title which translates as *"The Propagation of Innovation waves"*. It was at first based on ...kinetic gas theory, but some 12 years later, he published a new article in the European Journal of Sociology under the title *"A Monte Carlo Approach to Diffusion"*. He described the spread of improved grazing methods to control the spread of *bovine tuberculosis*. It was not the proximity of ...cows grazing together in a field, that taught people how the disease spread, but their owner's network of social contacts that spread the knowledge about an innovative method of safe grazing.

Not only the grazing of cows, but the quality of life in all countries depends on the rapid spread of inventions and innovations to reach every household - rich or poor. Technology needs to become accessible in price and location - distance - if the new devices offered for use or consumption by the people are to be diffused rapidly. Marketing as the intermediary between consumers and novel activities and products has a crucial role to play in raising peoples' standard of living. It should therefore be practiced and rapidly applied by the latest methods available.

The usual form of transmission of a new invention is by making it part of the 6.00 pm news on TV. Failing that, one has to resort to advertising and showing it any time and by any pretext on TV and distributing fliers about it. Inventing a novel cooking appliance could take months of research and several tests with various potential users - from housewives to professional chefs - before it is patented and placed on the market. Throughout the research and testing period, a careful watch has to be kept against spies planted by competitor companies, intent to steal ideas and secrets. If an invention has been made through sheer luck and the inventor - because of inexperience – has no idea as to how to patent it, it may be plagiarized to escape prosecution. Rather than carelessly boasting about it, the inventor should first apply to the Federal Ministry of Intellectual Property to patent it and then be prepared to prosecute any trespasser who does not pay him due royalties.

Inventions are often born in the course of conversations or consultations on related or even unrelated subjects. Just to encourage this kind of talk, some industrial and economically powerful nations have devised the technological think-tank complex named *"technopolis"* (Hall et al, 1994). The idea was born in "Silicon Valley", soon imitated in Ottawa as "Silicon Valley North" and multiplied by... 26 such cities in Japan. The European Union has some in Germany, France and Britain - and Russia cannot be far behind, as one early experiment is now counted as "history" but not a "failure".

Another recent idea is the "Virtual Corporation". The concept originated in Vermont, USA, where the amendment of a law, made the electronic transaction legal, if the corporation had an agent and a physical address in that state and grouped contractors working under profit sharing agreements. Immediately, administration, design and marketing services related to an innovative product were all possible through electronic transaction alone. A pioneer virtual corporation was Amazon.com, connecting buyers and sellers without overhead costs, real estate taxes, or other expenses.

NOTE ** SILICON is a gray metalloid (part metal) invented by Swedish chemist Jons Berzelius. It is now used for high-tech devices, especially computers in the form of 98% pure chips

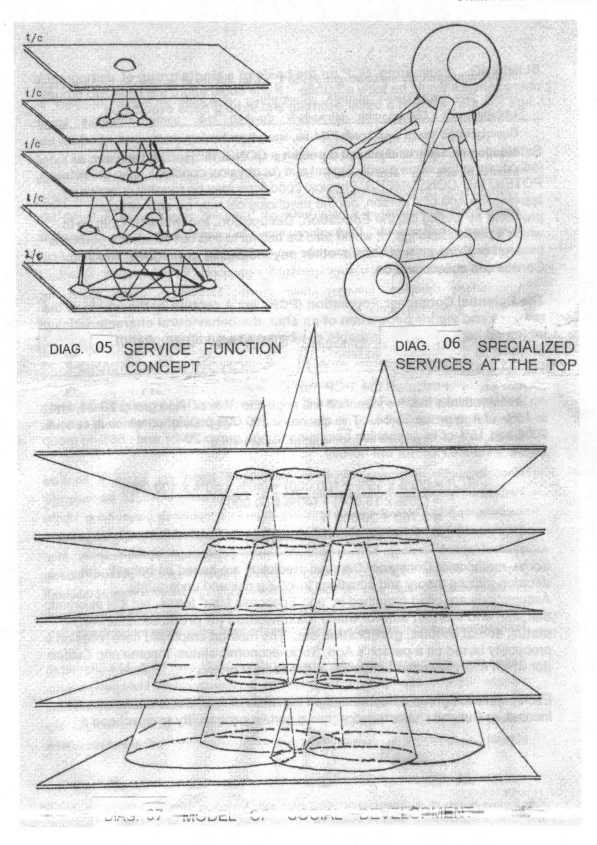

DIAG. 05 SERVICE FUNCTION
CONCEPT

DIAG. 06 SPECIALIZED
SERVICES AT THE TOP

DIAG. 07 MODEL OF SOCIAL DEVELOPMENT

3. THE BIRTH AND DEVELOPMENT OF SERVICES

Service industry is called "tertiary" in relation to Extraction and Manufacturing, but as far as creative, social and remunerative activity is concerned, Service has started earlier than the other two. It is inherent in family and collective life, because no human beings may be considered to live as a community, unless they consume the services rendered to each other. The prehistoric mother, for example, taking care of the needs of her new-born child and her hunter-provider husband, was surely the first person in society, to perform services.

SERVICE is an action performed in taking care of a need felt by other persons. The reward for this action may be an expression of love by the person(s) benefitting from the action, or responding with another service (e.g. husband hunting to supply food, or provide secure shelter and protection in return for services rendered by his wife). Mutual recognition of the value of the actions performed to each other was the birth of family life under a single shelter and later the birth of community life in a collective shelter – e.g. cave, long cabin, or stilted homes on a lake.

Services and facilities have been invented and will continue to be invented and developed throughout humanity's history, by reason of significant events which lead people to feel novel needs and demands or arrive at the resolution to put an end to an existing mode of an activity's operation and start anew. Fire for instance led to the formation of fire brigades and insurance companies; Injuries suffered by people led to the organization of hospitals; Earthquake led to structural innovations to allow greater stability and higher housing densities.

THE SERVICE FUNCTIONS CONCEPT (Diag. 05)

Every concept is based on a number of assumptions - statements which may be true at a given point in time and can "be used as foundations for reasoning the propositions which will follow them" (Popper, 1958). The assumptions underlying the Service Functions concept are as follows:-

A1. The spatial distribution of human activity reflects an adjustment to the friction of distance – considered in terms of space, time, price, social, economic and technological gaps between communities, travel time and cost;

A2. Location decisions aim to minimize the friction of distance;

A3. There is a tendency for human activities to agglomerate - for social and economic reasons;

A4. Advancing technology in the continuum of time, enables increasingly less focal - i.e. less densely concentrated - arrangements;

A5. Due to increasing mobility, urban life becomes a field phenomenon and it is best experienced in a city region offering a wide choice of activities;

A6. Common interests, rather than proximity are the basis of communal life;

A7. Ecology and culture are symbiotic and complementary.

The instinct of living together to ensure collective protection, hunting, safety and efficient performance of services for the community – e.g. lighting a fire to help all get warm. This was the root of collective life and society. The beginning of family life gave rise to nursing, education, play and recreation and the start of social life led to the management of human resources towards the organization of hunting, to leadership in joint effort for protection or aggression, to faith and worship. Not far behind came the early forms of exchange - presents, barter, trade and money.

Today, the above are known as welfare, education, recreation, professional services, administration, worship and commerce. Numerous subdivisions have been devised and developed in response to local circumstances, to technological change and especially to trends in fashion or custom.

NEED, DEMAND, CONSUMER and POTENTIAL CONSUMER

These four concepts have to be carefully defined, because when needs were not satisfied in a country or area in the past, protest and violent revolutions arose. Nowadays, protests against an insensitive government, turn to the United Nations Organization - for peace keepers, food supplies and shelter. Ensuring the highest quality of life for the greatest number, does not mean giving goods, food, or service without discretion. Counting people as grazing heads, with no discretion as to particular human needs - due to age, sex, education, income and cultural up-bringing has been the wrong - often a wilfully wrong diagnosis for centuries (Marie Antoinette's "Let them eat cake" for example, did not save her head). Discovering the factors making for differentiation of needs due to physical and psychological factors and recognition that demands are specific - rather than general - is the essence of the problem of supply. It leads to more accurate and fair allocation of resources and above all, avoids complaint, dispute protest, and the guillotine...

Consumer NEED is a function of personal values, physical, psychological and intellectual attributes; It is generated at the moment that news of an innovation reaches a person through conversation or visual, or social means - particularly TV adverts - and she or he feels that it could satisfy some requirement in his or her condition.

The moment the price is learned - the sacrifice in monetary, or other terms - and the person feels that he can afford it, the NEED becomes a DEMAND.

Consumer DEMAND is therefore a function of need, modified by considerations of the sacrifice of **POWER** for satisfying that need through an innovation or already known good, or service, or activity participation. This power is the capacity to buy, move, afford the time to do, have the influence to obtain, or be legally entitled to do or obtain, a good, service or activity participation to satisfy the need.

11

THE CONSUMER (Diag. 01)

The Consumer population of an area may be divided into categories on the basis of variations in consumer behaviour, in respect of goods, services and social activities. Census Canada provides information on several such categories, as follows:-

| AGE GROUPS: 0-14 ('kids'); 15-19 (teens); 20-24 (swingers); 25-44 (parents); 45-65 (liberated) 65+ (retired). |
| SOCIO-ECONOMIC. GROUPS: Professional wrkrs; Employers and Managers; Skilled tech wrkrs; Clerical wrkrs; Semiskilled wrkrs; Uskilled wrkrs. |
| ETHNIC GROUPS: First Nation; East Indian; Francophone; Anglophone; USA; Hispanic; European, Anzac, Middle-Eastern, East Asian; Oriental, S.E. Asian. |
| INCOME GROUPS: Less than $30k / annum; $30.1k- 50k; $50.1k-70k; $70k +. |
| MOBILITY GROUPS: No-car families; One-car families; Two-or-more car families. |

Each of these 31 demographic groups forms a distinct category of consumers, deserving the special attention of service and social activity managers. But in a brief guide to the busy entrepreneur searching for a market location, they are too detailed.

A selection of the most significant, reduced them to 16, as follows:-

Table 2: SELECTED 16 CONSUMER CATEGORIES

AGE GROUPS	S/E GROUPS	INCOME GROUPS	LANGUAGE GROUPS
0-19	Profess/Mang'l	$10-29k	English
20-24	Clerical workers	$30-49k	French
25-64	Skilled workers	$50-79k	Chinese
65+	Other workers	$80k+	Other

All of the above are proxies for consumer behaviour due to differences in physical and psychological conditions. These may be approximately guessed by finding out the age, socio-economic group, income and language of a person. Language is in fact, a proxy for several proxies (ethnic, educational, cultural, up-bringing, etc) all of them approximate, but nevertheless valuable for market research and location of outlets.

These 16 groups could be reduced further by asking the inventor of a product or service, which one or two of these characteristics are the most likely to become the decisive ones in determining his market. As shown on the fifth line of Diag. 01, the service or product often by its very name ("Ladies' tool box") makes it evident as to the category of consumer it is addressed to - by age, sex, income, or language. The shadings on Diag. 01 make also clear that consumers from parts of demographic bands may be interested in the Slimming course, set of Ladies' tools, Mutual fund shares, or an English novel. One has to discern the particular age, socio-economic category, income band and language group, in order to attract the supplier's attention, or focus an advertising campaign, select exhibition locations, etc.

THE POTENTIAL CONSUMER

When a person has purchased a product by exercising his taste, education, culture, etc, the satisfaction of his demand will make him or her a CONSUMER. Each consumer category however has a certain probability (from 0.0 to 1.00) of using a service which may be called a USE FACTOR. Multiplying all demographic groups by their use factors for a particular product or service, will give the POTENTIAL CONSUMER POPULATION **(PCP)** for that service or product. This may be defined as "Part or the whole of the resident and visitor population of an area, the behavioural characteristics of which make it the most probable consumer of a given innovation, service or product, at a particular time or season" (Armen, 1971).

The PCP for an innovation may be estimated on the basis of any number of consumer categories on which statistics are available or may be roughly determined by means of an ad hoc survey. Brief and approximate market location surveys for an innovation may suffice by finding just the age, occupation, language and income of potential consumers. The more attributes are investigated and used in the calculation, obviously the more accurate will the PCP estimate be. It is up to the inventor to determine the most decisive, because he had certain human needs in mind when he made the invention. It would be even safer to ask each buyer to state **how she or he will use** the novel product in her/his daily life or profession or other relevant attribute - her/his mother tongue and approximate income - and use these data to make a new PCP calculation. A re-assessment of advertising campaign, sales strategy and location of outlet may be necessary and this will result in greater savings and more sales.

A noteworthy case would be a compulsory law on education, requiring children between certain ages to attend school. Their probability of their attendance in that case would be 1.00 - i.e. certainty. Learning the age of a person may lead to a fairly accurate idea of his physical condition, but the psychological may be only remotely guessed by finding out also his education, occupation, culture and income. It would be helpful to find out whether a person is Introvert or Extrovert, but no census can collect that sort of sophisticated data.

EXAMPLE 1: FIND the PCP for A NOVEL SERVICE IN A CITY OF 100,000 PEOPLE

An inventor thinks that his invention will appeal to 25% of Age group 20-24, and to 40% of Age group 25-64. The city's population in Census 2006 had 15% of its population belonging to Age group 20-24 and 50% to group 25-64. Find the PCP for the novelty.

$$PCP = (25\% \times 15\% \times 100,000) + (40\% \times 50\% \times 100,000)$$
$$= (25\% \times 15,000) + (40\% \times 50.000)$$
$$= 3,750 + 20,000$$
$$= \underline{\textbf{23,750 potential consumers.}}$$

Some methods of consumer demand prediction are based on behavioural decision-making theory and on situations involving risk and uncertainty. Assumptions are often couched in "non-Economic Man" terms. Here, it is considered axiomatic that men and women aim for utility maximization (of profit, satisfaction, status, social welfare, gratification etc.). The method employed here (assuming a **probability** of purchase of a service or of an attendance of a public event), gives a satisfactory degree of accuracy for consumer prediction and market location purposes. When calculated as a correlation value between a consumer category and a service, it ranges from **.001** to **.999** - negligible to almost maximum use - and it is a convenient proxy for people's likes and dislikes, for an activity or service.

EXAMPLE 2: FIND the NUMBER and TYPES of schools needed in a CITY OF 100,000 people.

a. Assume the USE FACTORS of **.800** for Age group 3-10 to attend Day care and Primary schools; **.750** for Ages 10-14 to attend Secondary; and **.600** for Ages 15-25 years to attend College or University.

   In Census 2006 the percentages of these groups in the city were: 8%; 12%; and 16% respectively and therefore, the actual numbers of young people were 8,000; 12,000 and 16,000 respectively;

b. Multiplying these numbers by the appropriate Use Factors assumed above - 8,000 x .800 = **6,400;** 12,000 x .750 = **9,000;** and 16,000 x .600 = **9,600.**

   Taking the average number of students for a Primary, a High school and a College or University as 200; 260 and 10,000 students respectively, the schools required are therefore:-

32 day care + primaries; 4.6 (i.e.35) secondary schools; 1 College / University

THE DISTRIBUTION OF SERVICES

This is the paramount factor for the location of his innovation, but an inventor should also consider:-

(a) the existing distribution of associated services and social facilities and

(b) the environmental features of the area.

   These two will be referred to as System Location and Geographical Factors respectively and will be explained in the following two Sections.

Knowledge of the association between the services already existing in a city region and full awareness of the raw materials, products and clients required for his innovation to develop and thrive in that city region, will undoubtedly be a great help for the inventor or his agent looking for the best location for the innovation's first outlet. Existing service facilities may appear to be unevenly distributed in a selected region for the following reasons:-

• Persons in a consumer category are likely to spread unevenly;

• Consumer categories have unequal mobility means to reach services;

• Variations in accessibility, location advantages, topographical and climatic features will make some areas more suitable for some facilities than for others;

• Queuing effects in the process of diffusion of innovations will also cause departures from expected distributions;

• Variations are also created by historical accident favouring some places.

Due to all these factors, an apparently uneven distribution of **elements** (consumers, services, facilities and topographical features) will be generated, which may be called an elements distribution BIAS. All other things being equal, this brings about a tendency towards the specialization of an area in some services and its dependence in some others.

This interdependence of populated areas is in terms of the collective presence or absence of elements related to various aspects of human life in urban areas - shops, schools, playing fields, etc - and they form very functional groups - Commerce, Education, etc - in serving some aspect of human life in urban and rural areas. Such a group may therefore be called a SERVICE FUNCTION and has be studied in its composition.

If facilities form a functional system indeed, the links structuring them into a system, will also have to be proved. (Diags. 05 and 06)

PROOF OF LINKAGE BETWEEN THE ELEMENTS FORMING A SERVICE FUNCTION

When people visit a city to benefit from her services, they walk or drive from one outlet to another in an activity program linking all services or activities satisfying their needs during a shopping trip, or an entertainment outing, a journey or a holiday. All the facilities visited and the walks linking them form a system - a Service Function as defined above.

Existence of links between the constituent elements forming a functional system of services was proved by means of a correlations matrix based on city regions and various service and social activities in them.

EXAMPLE 3 : HOW LONG WOULD A MOVIE ON "Albert Einstein" BE PROFITABLE TO SHOW IN A CITY REGION OF 100,000 ?

a. Find out the proportion of people 14-80 years old in the city region. Let's say it was 65%. Therefore, the actual number of persons = **65,000**

b. Find out the percentage High school and University students in this number. Assuming 12% +16% = 28%. Therefore the total of students = 65,000 x 28% = = **18,200 students attending High school and University;**

c. Total number of people less students 65,000 -18,200 = **46,800;**

d. Assume a Use factor of **.600** for students and **.500** for people interested to attend, therefore = (18,200 x .600) + (46,800x .500) = 10,920 + 23400 = **34,320;**

e. If the audience accommodated in the hall = 800 per night = 34,320 / 800 = 42.75 say 43 nights
    = **6 weeks of profitable showing.**

THE CITY REGION

The field phenomenon of urban life may be best observed in environments which combine urban services at a level above small town or rural settlement activity. Census data indicate that cities above 45,000 - 50,000 population could be expected to have the essential characteristics of urbanity in terms of variety of services in early 21st century.

The attraction of a city's services will make the people from surrounding areas, travel to that city to purchase goods and enjoy urban facilities. Rural areas within convenient access to a city, together with that city, form a CITY REGION (Geddes, 1915). Green (1950) suggested city bus service hinterlands to delineate this region and Ratcliff (1955) studied such hinterlands and found that :-

i.   According to its level of specialization, each urban facility exerts an attraction across distance;

ii. This distance is more crucial in the dimension of time than actual distance;

iii. Specialized facilities attract the overwhelming majority of their clients from an area within 40-45 minute isochrones by public or private transport. Extending this limit to 60 minutes added only an insignificant number of further users (Min. of Transport, 1970).

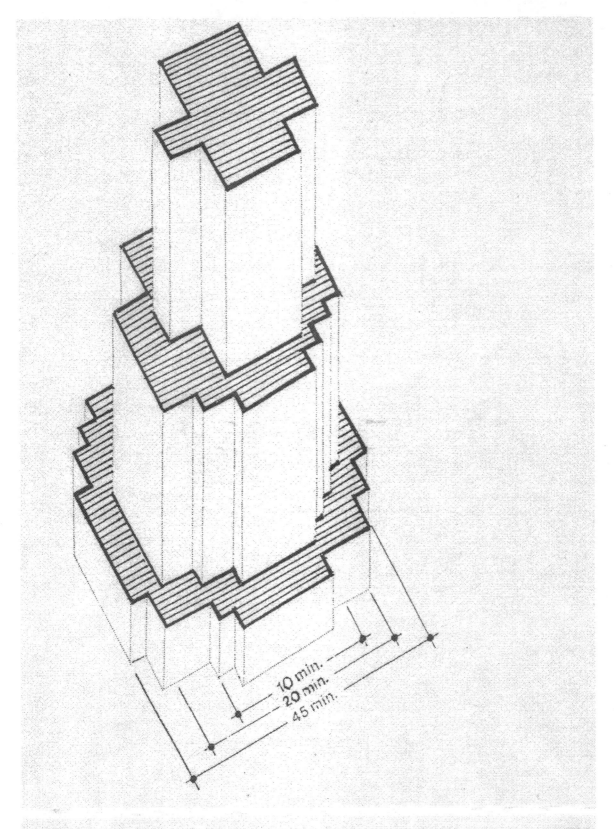

10 min.
20 min.
45 min.

DIAG. 08 SPECIALIZED SERVICE CATCHMENT ISOCHRONES

The city regions shown on Table 3 and Appendix "C" were drawn on the basis of a 40-45 minute isochrones from the main downtown cross roads in the city (Diag. 08). Access of service to client is continuously increasing, in parallel with advances in mobility and telecommunications. By 2020 the limit of 40--45 minutes will be considered to be far too long, as faster telecommunication and mobility become available.

The selection of city regions was guided by the assumption that city services imparting the enjoyment of urban life to entire regions, would be present in cities of at least 50,000 population, each considered as a continuously built-up area. A total of 49 such cities were listed, as shown below:-

Table 3: CITY REGIONS SELECTED FOR LINKAGE CALCULATION

1. Abbotsford (BC)	2 BarrieOrillia(ON)	3 Belleville(ON)
4. Calgary (AB)	5. Chatham-Kent (ON)	6. Charlottetown (PE)
7. Chilliwack (BC)	8. Drummondville (QC)	9. Edmonton (AB)
10. Fredericton(NB)	11. Granby (QC)	12. Halifax NS)
13. KitWatCamGul*(ON)	14. Kelowna (BC)	15. Kingston(ON)
16. Lethbridge(AB)	17. London (ON)	18. Medicine Hat (AB)
19. Moncton (NB)	20. Montreal (QC)	21. Nanaimo(BC)
22. Niagara-StCath (ON)	23. North Bay (ON)	24. Ottawa-Gatineau (ON)
25. Peterborough (ON)	26. Prince George (BC)	27. Quebec City (QC)
28. Saguenay QC)	29. Red Deer (AB)	30. Regina (SK)
31. St. John's (NL)	32. St. John (NB)	33. St. Hyacynth (QC)
34. Sarnia (ON)	35. Sault Ste Marie (ON)	36. Saskatoon (SK)
37. Sault Ste Marie (ON)	38. Sherbrooke (QC)	39. (Grtr) Sudbury (ON)
40. Sydney (NS)	41. Thunder Bay (ON)	42. Toronto (ON)
43. Trois Rivières (QC)	44. Kamloops (BC)	45. Kawartha Lakes(ON)
46. Windsor (ON)	47. Winnipeg (MB)	48. Vancouver (BC)
49. Victoria (BC)		

NOTE: * KitWatCamGul = Kitchener+Waterloo+Cambridge+Guelph

The above included the following variations:-

a) Inland cities at cross roads or other road junctions which had an extensive hinterland, as for example Prince George (BC) (see Appendix "C"); Fredericton (NB); and Winnipeg (MB). Numerically, their market depended on the number and residential density of urban and rural areas forming the city region.

b) Waterside cities like Halifax (NS), Barrie-Orillia (ON) and Nanaimo (BC) had their market areas curtailed but waterside benefits from tourism, transportation, holiday resort services, recreation and sailing - could very well exceed the profits of inland city regions;

c)   The capital of Prince Edward Island had an extensive agricultural hinterland, the seaside curtailment did not matter, as the holiday resort, tourism, sailing, boating, fishing and other profitable activities' amply compensated entrepreneur Islanders;

d)   A waterside or riverside megalopolis – Toronto, Vancouver, Montreal, Ottawa and Quebec city - had curtailed city regions due to severe congestion. The 40-45 min. isochrones failed to cover the built up area forming the megalopolis.

Entrepreneurs would therefore have to accept this curtailment of the market, but feel that the high residential density of the curtailed market, would amply compensate them for the number of distant clients lost or less frequently traveling to shop at the megalopolis downtown. Severe congestion and high land prices lead to suburban or out of town location.

None of these geographical variants was considered as limiting the validity of the 40-45 min. isochrones, on the basis of which the selected 49 city regions were drawn (Appendix "C"). An important criterion to bear in mind when comparing these city regions as markets is that although they may not look equal in land area, the WEALTH of residents and visitors is far more significant a factor than area.

THE CORRELATION MATRIX

This was the outcome of a mathematical operation which in effect, measured the number of times two elements were to be found together within a carefully defined area i.e. a city region and her surrounding settlements as defined above. A correlation value between a pair of elements arrayed on the vertical and horizontal axes of the matrix, indicated the strength of their relationship. The higher the correlation value, the stronger the link between the two elements - be they demographic groups, or services, or facilities, or environmental features or activities or any combination of these. If these elements relate to a large number of city regions and service outlets – rather than just a few - then the results will be valid at a high level of confidence.

Re-defining the variables and re-iterating the arguments for the variables selected for the calculation:-

LINKS were the streams of people or channels of things material and abstract, connecting elements to form the systems of Service Functions, which satisfy the consumer needs of the people living in CITY REGIONS. These are cities and surrounding settlements within 40-45 minute isochrones - contours of equal access points - to specialized SERVICES and FACILITIES providing the joys of city life as SERVICE FUNCTIONS. (All capitalized words formed the variables and outcomes of the correlation matrix to be formed and then analyzed).

VARIABLES entered on the horizontal and vertical axes of the matrix were-

(a)   The 49 city regions containing at least 50,000 people and offer the variety of urban activities and services their residents and visitors enjoy;

(b)   The 112 services, facilities and geographical features found in the city regions studied;

(c)   The 16 categories of consumers that form the clients of their services.

The matrix input data will thus consist of 49 city regions against the 16 consumer categories plus the 112 services and environmental features. All 128 types of data on consumers, facilities, services and environmental features were collected from census, city and town municipal guides and Yellow Page telephone directories.

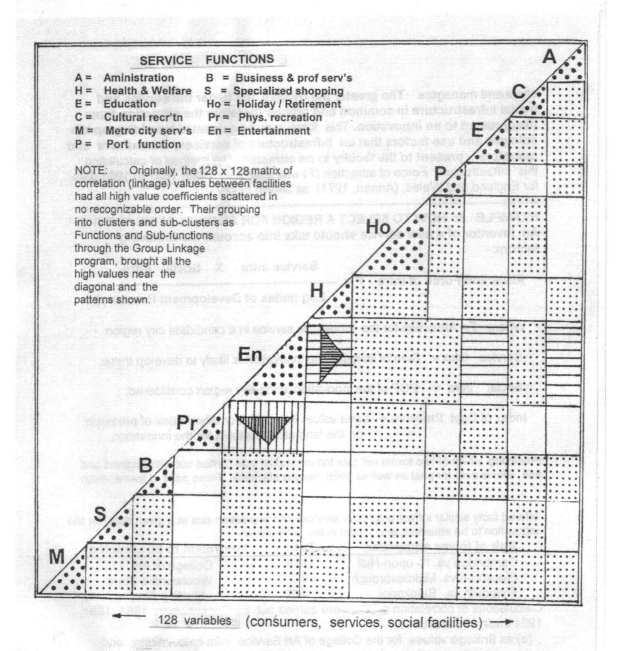

SERVICE FUNCTIONS

A = Aministration   B = Business & prof serv's
H = Health & Welfare   S = Specialized shopping
E = Education   Ho = Holiday / Retirement
C = Cultural recr'tn   Pr = Phys. recreation
M = Metro city serv's   En = Entertainment
P = Port function

NOTE: Originally, the 128 x 128 matrix of correlation (linkage) values between facilities had all high value coefficients scattered in no recognizable order. Their grouping into clusters and sub-clusters as Functions and Sub-functions through the Group Linkage program, brought all the high values near the diagonal and the patterns shown.

← 128 variables (consumers, services, social facilities) →

DIAG 09 SIMPLIFIED GROUP LINKAGE DIAGRAM

Dot triangles formed on the diagonal represent the highly specialized services while the arrows show the connected elements forming the

RESULTS

A total of 128 types of elements - facilities, services and consumer categories - were listed for each of these city regions and the correlation matrix formed had therefore 128 x 128 data cells, yielding 16,384 correlations. The numerical value of each matrix term indicated the strength of a relationship and the most significant were between:-

a. **People with Service activities** indicating the close connection between the residential location of demographic categories of people and service outlets they use from day to day. Among the services included were the major shopping center 'magnets'- Sears, The Bay, Wal-Mart, etc.

b. **People with Place links** give a clue as to the geographical features preferred for residential location by each of the 16 demographic categories selected.

c. **People with People links** describe the polarization of various demographic groups by choice, or force of circumstance. This element of choice allows the sociologist to select interesting research subjects as to motivation, affinity, no-choice forced on some groups when it comes to residential location. Social area analysis carried out by Park & Burgess (1925), led to the ecological approach and the conclusion that "Birds of a feather, flock together". This is particularly significant for services as well as housing developments, as it makes for easier prediction of demands for areas inhabited by 'flocking' demographic groups and for easier choice of housing types to build in each area. Both services and housing may be built with the confidence that all services and homes will meet with assured consumption.

d. **Service with Service** and - **Facility with Facility** links indicating the location preferences of their managers to facilitate the exchange of things material (raw and manufactured) as well as abstract (prestige, telecommunications, etc).

On plotting the city region markets of the selected 49 cities, it was found that about 65% of the population of the 10 southern Provinces (Diag. 02) and no less than 90% of the population in the Golden Horseshoe (Diag. 04) had been included in the city regions studied.

The most significant outcome from the marketing point of view however, were the systems of 10 SERVICE FUNCTIONS shown in Appendix "A". Each pyramid of services, facilities, institutions, operator-and-consumer categories shows the total number of elements to be found in a fully developed Service Function, in a city region. A newly developing Function like Tourism may be based on an existing Cultural, Specialized shopping, Entertainment, or Holiday/Retirement Function - whichever facilities are predominant. In 10 years' time when all Canadian elements (services, facilities, etc.) have been further developed, these Functions will have acquired more specialized elements at the top, while many lower level elements will have disappeared due to redundancy.

The 10 current Service Functions were derived by applying the Linkage Analysis program (R. Ng, 1969) summarized as a diagram (09). This calculation-and-matrix processing assembled the highest correlation values into triangles formed on the diagonal of the matrix. The arrows pointing horizontally and vertically, show lesser associations of each Function with sections of other Functions.

Correlation values are proxy linkage values, because among things previously mentioned, they indicated above all, the exchange of clients. While a low correlation indicated few instances of client exchange, a high value showed that in most city regions, the two facilities or services operated symbiotically to make a living and create wealth for their operators. It could be argued that any two variables could have been located in the same city region by pure chance. But if they were together in 48 out of 49 times, they probably had a functional relationship which included economic interdependence - e.g. couple enjoying a night out by having a restaurant meal and then going to the cinema nearby. A much more profitable relationship would be between a restaurant and the Stock Exchange, with clients or brokers meet in the former and go to trade in the later.

According to statistical tables of Student's 't' values, a minimum correlation of **.240** could be considered reliable at 99.9% confidence level, if it has been computed from at least 100 variables. In this case they had been computed from 128 and therefore any value above **.240** could be considered reliable.

The lower level elements of each pyramid shown in Appendix "A", form the INFRASTRUCTURE of that Function. The more of these elements are present in a city region, the more powerful will be the attraction of that region to any of the absent specialized elements in the Function's SUPERSTRUCTURE above. An innovation related to that superstructure by virtue of potential links with existing elements within 45-minutes' access, will also be strongly attracted to that city region. This Force of attraction (F) was established with 1861 to 1966 data for England and Wales, (Armen, 1971) as shown below:-

EXAMPLE 4: HOW TO SELECT A REGION FOR AN INNOVATIVE SERVICE

The inventor of a new service should take into account the following factors:-

$$\text{Attraction Force of Infra F} = \frac{\textbf{Service infra X Social infra}}{\textbf{Log (Index of Devel't Pressure)}}$$

Where F = Attraction for the innovative service in a candidate city region;
Service infra = Sum of linkages the innovation is likely to develop there;
Social infra = PCP+0perators of the innovation in the city region considered;
Index of Development Pressure = Land value, Population size or other index of pressure on the land area available for the innovative service.

Predicting which of two towns will gain the innovation was carried out with England & Wales data for 1841 to 1966 Census statistics. Three pairs of towns which offered fairly similar infrastructures of services and population size at a given date, for the innovation to be attracted, are shown in the table below:-

Towns competing	Date	Innov'n to be attracted
Cambridge vs Kingston-upon-Hull	1858	College of Art
Blackburn vs Middlesborough	1920	Woolworth's Store
Plymouth vs. Blackpool	1963	Bowling Alley

Garbis Armen, BA, MRTPI, PhD

Calculations of correlation values were carried out for Census years 1861, 1891, 1921 and 1966 to compute:

(a) Linkage values for the College of Art service infra;

(b) Use factors for socio-economic groups for social infracture and were assumed to be valid for the dates shown on the table above (1858, 1920 and 1963) and the following two arrays were formed :-

Innovation to be attracted:- COLLEGE OF ART			
Linked facilities in CAMBRIDGE		ditto in KINGSTON-on-HULL	
Theatre	.021	Theatre	.021
Rail station	.013	Rail station	.013
University	.668	Local newsp'r	.102
Museum	.380	Botanical gdns	.313
Public Library	.011	Public Library	.011
Courts	.045	Courts	.045
Serv. infra	**1.138**	**Service infra**	**0.505**

Similar tables were formed for the **Social infrastructures** offered by Cambridge and Hull to attract a College of Art. The totals of Service and Social infrastructures were **3.216 and 3.109 respectively.** As regards the Index of Development Pressure, population of the respective town on the nearest Census date was considered to be a satisfactory **proxy for the Development pressure on land.** Thus the Log Index for Cambridge (1861 population = 76,520) was **4.803** and for Hull, with a population of 86,890 was **4.939.** Using the figures for each town in the equation, the results were:-

F (Cambridge) = 1.138 x 3216 / 4.803   F (Hull) = 0,505 x 3109 / 4.939

F (Cambridge) = 761.9   **F (Hull) = 317.9**

College of (Art built: 1858   **College of Art built: 1861**

Similar calculations to compare the Forces of each of the other pairs of towns indicated the Woolworth's Store as being attracted earlier to Middlesborough and the Bowling alley to Blackpool. Canadian examples may be worked out when appropriate historical data on dates of innovation arrivals in various towns are available to carry out the necessary calculations. Unfortunately, no census was carried out in Canada until 1871 and the scope for such retroactive studies is more limited. Telephone directories and town guides came much later than 1871.

Local surveys of facilities and services within easy access would be useful when considering an out of town location and comparing it with a downtown alternative. The great contrast in accessibility to facilities and services will be evident in the "**F**" value.

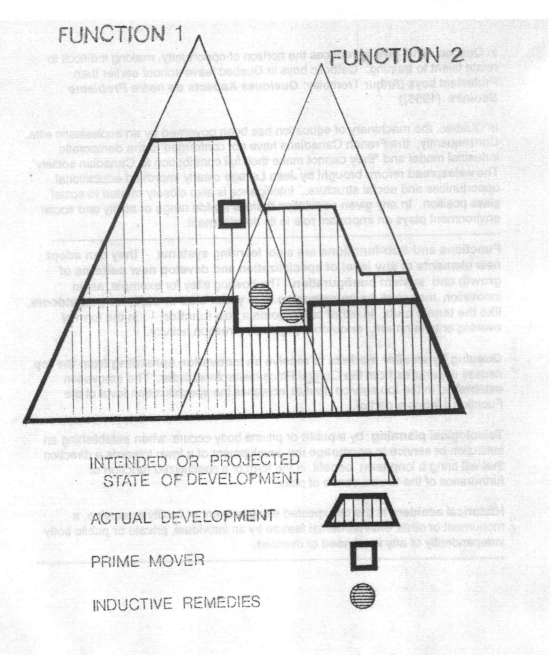

FUNCTION 1

FUNCTION 2

INTENDED OR PROJECTED
STATE OF DEVELOPMENT

ACTUAL DEVELOPMENT

PRIME MOVER

INDUCTIVE REMEDIES

DIAG. 10: MONITORING AND CONTROL OF DEVELOPMENT

The superstructure at the top of a Function are highly specialized facilities which are strongly linked through the exchange of things material (clients, etc) and abstract (prestige, etc). An Olympic swimming pool and a University at the top of the Physical Recreation Function for example will have many clients in common and the closer their spatial relationship, the greater the benefit to both. Other top facilities gain by reason of proximity at the most appropriate geographical location for them. This may be a port, a swimming beach, a mountain resort, or a new technopolis (Hall et al 1994).

QUALITIES AND USES OF THE SERVICE FUNCTIONS CONCEPT

1. As a building development and congestion control means

Service Functions as organisms consisting of elements like services, facilities, activities and above all people - as consumer and operators - form a very significant system for controlling the development of city regions. Positive or negative outcomes - whichever considered beneficial for the short or long term development of a town -may be achieved by controlling the spatial relationship, phasing and deliberate establishment or removal of the elements forming a Service Function. This may best be carried out by "Cybernetic control", defined as "A method of securing an intended outcome of a sequence of actions - or chain of facilities - which are known to be associated, by controlling the early phases of the sequence". This definition is derived from the Greek word 'kyvernitika' and not from Barrett's 1996 *"State of the Cyber nation"*. If municipal officers would exercise cybernetic control, fewer developers in their area would wait for slow Council decisions, or get angry with the municipal officers. A positive move by the British Columbia Provincial authorities for example, was to spread the venues of Winter Olympic Games, throughout the Vancouver megalopolis to avoid possible unmanageable congestion in Whistler.

The opportunity often arises for a municipality to exercise positive development control by stimulating development in a strategic direction that conforms with the Council's plan, or encourages an Entrepreneur by accelerating the approval of his scheme and providing supplementary public facilities - from street lights and sewers to new schools and clinics to satisfy consumer demand arising from new families attracted by the Entrepreneur's housing estate. This is not favouring the Entrepreneur, but minimizing the waiting time for public facility provision and possible suffering of new residents.

Diag. 10 illustrates how a prime mover may be used to further the development of a selected Service Function towards greater specialization, more effectively, than by building inductive remedies.

2. As a means of analyzing and understanding urban or rural character

Social and economic effects of the presence of service and social facilities in a city region are part of everyday experience and economy. People meet and socialize in pubs, get to know their neighbours in shops, chat with them in clubs and other social facilities or they are employed in retail services, in primary schools as teachers and in universities to earn the family's upkeep. It is in these schools that all young men and women come to the early realization of their talents and reach the stage of college and university entry to develop these talents as professionals.

At a particular level of technological and cultural development of a country, the layout of a Service Function's elements have significant effects not only on the social and economic, but also on the environmental character of an urban or rural settlement - her attraction to tourists for visits at the most appropriate season and to entire families for permanent residence.

The frequency of contacts between facilities and people - as consumers or operators - determines how valid is the membership of a facility to a Service Function. Over time, some facilities tend to become redundant, unless they evolve to conform with changing consumer habits according to fashion. The total number of contacts between a pair of facilities provides a measure of their interdependence and of the possibility of their producing synergetic effects - i.e. outcomes beyond expectation.

3. As a means of understanding the qualities of various elements

Examination of the strength of linkages between facilities forming a Function at a progressively more stringent levels of significance, will eliminate feeble links liable to severance in times of economic or other crisis. Severance of feeble links will isolate small groups of facilities which may be called sub-functions.

Functional systems possess a **memory** - they reproduce earlier patterns of development activity, if the appropriate stimulus returns. This may be in the form of a financial grant, a change in Federal or Provincial taxation policy, the appearance of an enthusiastic leader, or an unexpected innovation, which may accelerate urban or specialized service development as a prime mover (Diag. 11). Prime movers provide a stimulus to a Function's or Sub-function's further development not only upwards - towards the acquisition of new consumers and specialized elements - but also in the direction of that Function's broadening the range of facilities to serve more varied and broadly sophisticated consumers at the catchment level of the Prime Mover.

Functions and Sub-functions are **learning systems** - they can adopt new elements at any level of specialization and develop new patterns of growth and system configuration. The bowling alley for example, as an innovation, may start as an extension of a youth club or café, or go into a separate building, or outdoors, like the tennis club. In either case it joins a new function - as a form of evening entertainment, or outdoor physical recreation activity.

Queuing by smaller markets to receive an innovation spreading from the top, causes departures from the Central Place hierarchical order (Diag. 12). An innovation established in the top market increases the specialization level of the Function it forms a part of (Thomas, J.,1968).

Teleological planning occurs when an institution, a public body, a benefactor, or a Council capable of taking a long-term view of a city's future, provides the finance for the development of a Service Function in a direction that will bring a long term benefit to the city. It may lead to a specialization, or the growth of a particular form of tourism, or an increase in overseas trade, or the development of a 'sense of place' (Section 4).

Historical accident is the unexpected establishment of a facility, or service, or Monument, or other environmental feature, by an individual, private or public body, independently of any local need or demand.

SIGNIFICANCE OF THE EDUCATION FUNCTION

A broad prime mover for society as a whole is the Education system, for which only 5.2 % of Canadian GDP is allocated. Exemplary were the changes made in the English educational system in 1944, providing free education all the way to university and marking the start of great economical development in UK. In USA there has always been a strong force in favour of equality in educational opportunity. In Canada however, there is no national educational system because there are no fewer than 11 systems - one for each Province and one for the Territories controlled by the Federal government. Was the objective behind the British North America Act to Balkanize the country? Time to reform Canada's Constitution (now in Ottawa) and become "Masters in our own house".

An equitable distribution of adequate schools extends the boundaries of employment by helping children acquire marketable skills. For decades Canada has imported a large number of skilled and professional workers (Porter, 1965) to reach the level of present economic development. An industrial economy requires a freely moving labour force - not a caste system of inherited jobs from kin as in Pakistan. Should education be made equally available to all, careers would be truly open to the talented and the meritorious. This egalitarian ideology comes into conflict with the structure of class (Porter, 1965). Inequality of income makes education expensive and greatly reduces the horizon of opportunity, making it difficult to relate talent to training.

Catholic boys in Quebec leave school earlier than Protestant boys (Tremblay 1956). The machinery of education has been governed by an ecclesiastic elite. Consequently, French Canadians have not conformed to the democratic industrial model and "they cannot make their full contribution to Canadian society" (Porter, 1965). The widespread reform brought by Premier Jean Lesage clearly improved educational opportunities and social structure. Intelligence is also closely related to social class position. In any given population there is a wide range of ability and social environment plays an important role in its development.

4. ON SPECIALIZATION AND SENSE OF PLACE

During the early stages of its diffusion, an innovation counts as a highly specialized commodity by virtue of its rarity. The definition of specialization in this context would be "The rarity and degree of sophistication it caters for, in a particular realm of social or service interest". As shown on Diag. 06 and Appendix "A", a proxy for the scale of specialization for service outlets is the number of people forming their catchment. Out of a large catchment however, only a few can afford to buy that specialized service or product. All things rare are more expensive, appeal to the richer, more educated, more refined in taste, more outgoing, exhibitionist types of person. It is certainly more profitable to trade in more specialized goods and traders of a particular good tend to locate close to each other to benefit from commensalism - the reinforcement of appeal when related establishments in proximate location collectively appeal to the consumer (Rannells, 1956).

SPECIALIZATION OF AN AREA is "The systematic variation of characteristics producing a unison of people, place and activities towards the effective performance of a function in relation to neighbouring and distant areas". An important implication of a specialization is the development of a "SENSE OF PLACE: a feeling conveyed by the scenes, sounds and smells one experiences in an area, giving the impression that the people, environmental features and activities seen or taking place, are all tuned towards the performance of a particular function". (Armen, 1971, 1972).

This definition differs vastly from the "Genius loci" which emperor Augustus turned "from a cult to a worship". Incredibly, a relief depicting this jargon, has survived on a wall of St. Giles church in the obscure village of Tackenham, in Wiltshire, UK (Google). Interpreted as "spirit of a place" it has found adherents in landscape design and architecture, where it means a faith in vernacular forms, free of cosmetic detail; A magical entity enveloping a space; Topophilia; Cultural geography; Ecological landscape.

The attraction of associated facilities around the pioneering service outlet offering an innovation, generates - by virtue of links developing between facilities - a novel Service Function and sometimes, the entire neighbourhood becomes known by that Function, attracting further associated activities, consumers and especially tourists.

"Once observed, analyzed and appreciated, this specialization could become a basis for the reinforcement of character and of complementary relationships between a community and surrounding settlements - a development which might help it to acquire an identity and a role in relation to them." (Armen, 1971)

Prince Edward Island's 2006 population for example, was 136,851. Capital Charlottetown's "Trading area" was given as 58,000 (Census 2006), but the city's hinterland is much larger and her catchment considerable. It is a large agricultural city region with a particular tourist attraction, as proven by the coach-loads of Japanese tourists attracted by the cottage of "Green Gables". In addition to selling souvenirs to them the region is an ideal market for tractors and agricultural machinery. It certainly has a "sense of place".

Toronto, Ottawa and many Canadian cities - large or small - are famous for their ethnic markets from Chinatown to Greektown and from Corso Italia to Koreatown. These ethnic markets often start as daring adventures by newcomer immigrants venturing to sell imports from the 'old country'; They soon develop a clientele - and once a market gets an ethnic name, the catchment grows, specialization in ethnic foods expands and the market becomes popular with Canadians in general (Armen, 1975). Smells are most evocative of childhood memories and added to the colours and tastes, they make the foods offered attractive not only to ethnic clients, but to a great many Canadians too. Every ethnic market has a character and a sense of place of its own - smells, sounds and even sensibilities of grocers about their "non-touchable" merchandise...

DEVELOPMENT OF SPECIALIZATION IN A CITY REGION

The development of a Specialized Function in service activity is shown in Diag. 06, indicating that with the passage of time (t) and addition of consumers (c) in a city region, outlets of a service multiply and more specialized facilities and products are added, as clients ask for more, consume more and expect greater sophistication in both services and products.

Diag. 05 and Appendix "A" show the superstructure of a Service Function fully developed to cater for the demands of a progressively more sophisticated catchment (Diag 08) the isochrones being based on a cross-roads where many of the facilities of the Function's superstructure are located, are rectilinear. This superstructure stands on a service and social infrastructure - the lower levels of services, the operators and consumers. Uniting Diags. 06 and 08 into a cone, the group of Functions forming a city region (Diag. 07) including outdoor facilities, beaches and ski resorts becomes an assembly of cones showing a **"Model of a region's social development"** because it sums up the total of social and service activity developed over centuries of life in a city region (Armen, 1971).

The inclination of each cone representing a Function in Diag. 07 indicates the direction of future prospects in specialization of the city region. It is up to inventors, entrepreneurs, benefactors and local municipality officials to dream what new service or facility they could promote to help that specialization develop further. The word "dream" may sound inappropriate in a practical guide to the selection of market location, but dreaming is indeed every inventor's habit towards a NEW invention. Only in dreams, in "virtual images" and imagination does an inventor see the first vision of his invention. And then the thrill of that vision, tends to push him towards hard work, experimentation and eventually, to the realization of his invention. The mass production of every item invented and brought for sale on a market and eventually on the world market for the benefit of humanity is often very costly and left to others. The inventor and his successors will have to be satisfied by cashing the royalties for the invention.

Every invention / service / activity tends to reach a peak in popularity and then, through change of fashion due to novel technological developments, events, fashion and new habits, starts to decay towards redundancy - a recurring, continual process in human history. Examples abound all around us, the cinema being a fairly recent one, due to the emergence of TV and DVD. Some economical reason is always involved, because the new invention or substitute, comes at a lower price - all as part-and-parcel of the process. But the sad outcomes are bankruptcies, the closing down of outlets, the end of outmoded products and professions.

Good municipal governance in temporary charge of a city's future, could counteract to this sad decline in the urban fabric by following principles, which have proved viable worthwhile objectives in many cities, large and small:-

1. Diverse and financially affordable long-term choices;

2. Strong and diversified service and manufacturing economy;

3. Optimized use of natural assets without depletion or land scars;

4. Compact, continuous and socially viable urban structure;

5. Sustainable urban public transport system, offering two choices;

6. Pride in well-preserved green, yet usable recreation areas;

7. Flexible zoning, open to the market, to enterprise and the unexpected.

HIERARCHICAL AND FEDERAL MODELS OF REGIONAL DISTRIBUTION

Throughout Canada's and USA's history, town sizes and distribution depended on

(a) The westward migration of European immigrants to grow larger; and

(b) The discovery of scarce and valuable resources - gold, oil, uranium, etc.

Population density in Europe however, was quite high, as in South Germany. That is where W. Christaller carried out his research and in 1933 published his Central Place theory, which attracted much study and criticism by many geographers (Jones, 1966). Christaller 's basic assumptions were as follows:-

1. The spatial distribution of human activities reflects an adjustment to the factor of distance - considered as space, time, income, value, as well as sociological, economic and technological gaps between one place and another;

2. Location decisions seek to minimize the frictional effects of distance;

3. Some locations are more accessible than others;

4. Due to the social genes of human species, human activities tend to agglomerate. Men and women favour the concentration of elements at accessible common locations;

5. The diffusion of ideas and goods proceeds from a focus to the periphery. (Machiavelli, 1531);

6. The dense packing of circular hinterlands produces a pattern of regular hexagons (von Netterdorf, 1809);

7. The organization of human activity is essentially hierarchical - in spatial and non-spatial aspects. In central place theory, Christaller (1933) states that "The chief profession of a town is to be the centre of a region".The study of deviations from this theory has attracted a large volume of research (Jones, 1964), the principal deviations being -

8. Provision of a service good has a population threshold of profitability and the hierarchy of such thresholds is stepped (Turgot, 1844); This has been disputed by Vining (1953) who believes in a continuum of thresholds and profitability;

9. The number of services performed by a city will vary in direct relation to the population it serves in her city region ;

10. Innovations diffuse uniformly down the hierarchy of centres.

11. As settlements become larger, they add fewer functions for each additional increment of population size (Berry & Garrison, 1958A).

Christopher Alexander (1966) in his devastating critique of central place theory titled "A City is Not a Tree" has pointed out that a hierarchical structure makes many new communities vulnerable to traffic congestion, because it causes all service journeys to be directed to the centre. He contrasted this state of one-and-only choice in things to do and places to go in new communities, with natural towns and cities, which are full of surprises, rather than being utterly predictable. The city, he concluded, is rich with overlap, its structure is complex - not a simple tree."

The earliest observation of a complex structure at work was given by Burton (1963). In Ontario, USA, Germany and Britain, he observed groups of cities which appeared to work as a single urban service unit, with people traveling to each for different functions. He formulated the Dispersed City Hypothesis in loose terms because according to Haggett (1965) 'Working definitions of the specialist centre are still lacking'. What is clear is that specialist centres in a regional context do not conform to the Central Place Hierarchy postulated by Christaller, but to a federal model of distribution, whereby towns interact on the basis of specialization. This contrasts sharply with the postulates of Central Place theory, being based on the following assumptions, (continuing from 11 above);-

12. There is a continuum through time;

13. Advancing transport and communications technologies allow an increasing 'affocality' in urban life and dispersal of services (being located out of town);

14. Urban life is increasingly a "field phenomenon" and not an exclusive 'central place' attribute;

15. Rather than the traditional family ties, or physical proximity, the basis of 'friendship nowadays is based on a community of interests held in common';

16. The realms of human activity form a continuum from the local to the global;

17. People differ by the number of realms of activity they embrace.

Assumptions 8 to 18 above are implicit in the Service Functions concept (Diags.05, 06) and the Model of Social Development. They are based on Consumer demand, System location, Geographical variation of location advantages, queuing effects in the Distribution of services, teleological planning and historical accident in the acquisition of Institutions or loss of services as in times of an economic recession.

5. DEVELOPMENT AND DECLINE OF SPECIALIZATION

Service Functions involving services, facilities, activities and above all, people - as operators and consumers - are the lifeblood of city regions. And as live organisms, they grow and thrive in sophistication when prospects for all constituent elements are good, or they decline and die, when they are bad.

Favourable prospects may be evident in every growing city region, but almost deceptive are the unfavourable ones. Changes in the urban scene are often imperceptible because both growth and decline work rather gradually in a multitude of elements, affecting them gradually and elastically. A restaurant owner calling his young son to help with potato peeling, or table-waiting, or helping unload the family SUV after a shopping trip, can hardly be called 'growth of the Entertainment Function'. Conversely, when the same restaurant owner, feeling the weight of an economic crisis, releases his less senior waiter from employment, feeling unable to recommend him to some other restaurant - thát is a small, but definite sign of decline in the Entertainment Function.

EFFECTS OF POLITICAL CHANGE ON SERVICE FUNCTIONS

One of the most influential factors on the prospects for Service Functions is the financial policy of any tier of government. The National government is the most influential with its tax levels, followed closely by the Provincial and lastly by Local government. One might wish for urban and rural services - particularly the ones related to Welfare, Education and Physical recreation - were legislated in ways that would make successive governments, unable to change them casually, according to political ideology, whimsy or narrow economical approach. But it is worth considering the effect of each type of change so that minimal permanent suffering to citizens or damage to the built environment results. Here are some hypothetical changes and their likely effects:-

Administrative functions employment at national level could be reduced by any Government wishing to save funds and curtail the bureaucracy in general - in pursuance of its political ideology, savings, or other objective. Curtailing the bureaucracy will always create some unemployment. Regional and municipal governments could also reduce employment by curtailing the corresponding levels of administration.

Health facilities - from doctors' surgeries and clinics to hospitals - could be severely affected by economic austerity measures of the Federal government. Higher level facilities dependent on Federal government grants, would receive some relief as soon as newspapers show long waiting queues and even deaths of waiting patients. Temporary shortages on local facilities run by

Municipal or Provincial governments could be more easily overcome. Technological progress through innovations - Magnetic Resonance Imaging in hospitals for example - could cause waiting queues before benefactors donate funds to ensure that such innovations become available to regional and even ordinary hospitals for the treatment of patients. Local welfare societies would also organize public collections of money to overcome such hospital and health service shortages.

Social Welfare, pensions and old age security systems have been subject to political manipulation ever since their foundation[1] (*). They may not give rise to many facilities on the ground, but as the proportion of aged people is continuously increasing, any government that dares to reduce their budget, will suffer in the ballot boxes.

Education is highly vulnerable to Provincial restriction of funds. Inequality of income makes education expensive for the large and poor family – particularly as in Quebec. This greatly reduces the horizon of opportunity, making it difficult to relate talent to training. Catholic boys in Quebec leave school earlier than Protestant boys (Tremblay, A, 1956) sometimes without reaching an understanding of their own talents.

Cultural recreation facilities are particularly vulnerable to economic upheavals and technological innovations. Other than the theatre, which from ancient times has been active in any town or city worth its salt, libraries have depended on municipal pride for their provision and maintenance. When budgets are tightened, libraries tend to become multi-purpose halls. Art Galleries, whether municipal or private, crucially depend on local prosperity and many small towns can afford to have just one, through private benevolence - for which there is a substantial tax deduction to gain. Art galleries, museums and libraries tend to diminish in size or number during a severe financial crisis. Politics, technological innovations, computers, video films and automatic translation devices - could also reduce the number of visits to cultural facilities.

Physical recreation facilities are increasing in types and number, as technology brings forth innovations in flying, diving, parachuting, ballooning, or even skating devices. Flying clubs increase in parallel with the building of aerodromes, just as sport and transportation venues tend to increase in Canada, because of long travel distances. Tight economic times tend to cause reductions in their use for sport, though less for transportation.

Entertainment services operate independently of government funds, but they are sensitive to financial austerity measures affecting the clients' pocket. Cinemas are gradually becoming weekly bingo halls but they may return to full-time movie showing when things improve. Variety theatres and betting shops have almost disappeared, but social clubs crop up in practically every locality.

Retail trades as the first venture of many newcomers to Canada are thriving, but in times of recession are also the first to close down. Advantageous locations on a Main street or a shopping mall are the only places to survive. Technology brings about more sophisticated vending machines,

---

1   Earliest user of Social Welfare for a political objective was Otto von Bismarck (1815-1898), who as Prussia's conservative prime minister, did not hesitate to introduce a Social Security system (1862) to win the favour of German workers . After reinforcing the Zollverein customs union (1834) between German principalities to foster trade and industry and unite them to capture Schleswig-Holstein from Denmark (1864) then defeat Austria in the Seven weeks' war (1866), he formed and led the German Confederation against France, (having notoriously edited the Elms Telegram which precipitated the war 1870-71). As first Chancellor of the German Reich, he succeeded in forestalling the rise of socialism by increasing Social Security of German workers. Hitler copied his welfare strategy to increase Nazi party membership. His admiration was evident in naming the largest WWII German warship, "Bismarck", which was sank by W. Churchill's order near the coast of Brazil.

but will never eliminate the friendly neighbourhood fruit-and-veg retailer. At the other end of the scale, superstores are likely to continue growing and causing the small shopkeeper to give up his trade. Their large car parks will have to be carefully landscaped to prevent eyesores in the urban and rural scene.

Financial advisor offices may be expected to grow in future as the ordinary citizen increasingly looks to shares and investment places to augment his earnings.Such offices are also sensitive to financial crises.

Transport nodes like airports, rail stations, bus stations and bus stops depend on government decisions which are forthcoming in times of prosperity, or recede in times of financial crisis. Bus stops are most likely to stay, regardless of crises.

Special events at national and international level - Olympic Games, Festivals and International Fairs / Conferences - could also be used by governments at all levels to boost up development, gentrification and landscaping, simply to extend their popularity and prestige. It is not unheard also, to drastically reverse the development trend after the special event, by closing down other facilities - like schools - instead of increasing taxes to reduce debts. Such an increase often means loss of votes.

CONCLUSION: Service Functions may develop or decline in a spasmodic fashion in response to financial growth or decline. While governments may initiate a trend either way, entrepreneurs have to keep alert and abreast with their plans to expand or start new outlets for particular service and social facilities.

"SENSE OF PLACE" DEVELOPING IN AN AREA

The potential for this sense developing when the site for an innovative facility is being selected, should naturally be taken into consideration, by using any feature that appears to be exceptional - mountain top, seaside beach, or river bend - will delight a gifted architect inspired by that feature. If the initiator of that facility - whether a private or public body - is also prepared to spend the estimated amount, the sense of place will soon develop. It takes foresight and effort, but little extra money if it is wisely designed.

A specialized facility created in an attractive location related to its function will tend to collect many subsidiary facilities. The specialized facility will act as a prime mover and a synergetic relationship will soon develop between all of them - a relationship that will attract more clients for the group, year after year and they will thrive in growing profits. Such was the case with Davos after the first World Economic Forum took place there. Hotels, ski recreation facilities restaurants, and entertainment and followed and the place developed as a unique conference centre and tourist resort.

In 1213 "Tavaus" was just a village at a rather inaccessible height of 1560 metres. Today, it is called Davos and it is the heighest city in Europe with a native 2008 population of barely 11,142. Height, snow and ski slopes were the physical resources, but what made the city famous was an initiative taken in 1971, by an economics professor of the University of Geneva, Klaus Schwab. He invited 444 executives from all over the world to hold an economic forum at the local conference hall. He explained to them an invention of his - the "Stakeholder" management approach, involving producers, managers and clients — all of them shareholders of the same company. A World Economic Forum was founded and by 1974, some political leaders were also invited. Research reports that the permanent staff produced on the Economy, Health and the Environment, as well as papers like "Creative Capitalism" by Bill Gates' became prime reading material in many developed countries all over the world. Famous meetings - as for the reconciliation between Greece & Turkey, South Africa's Mandela & Klerk - were held and successfully resolved through "Davos Declarations". In January each year, thousands of tourists swelled the growing number of hotels and it became a habit to visit the seven Swiss national heritage sites in Davos, then to ski and go to the spas after the forums had been held. Today, Davos is Europe's largest ski resort and ice hockey tournament site.

In the case of **Bristol,** a series of teleological actions and historical accidents brought the outcome of one of the busiest ports in UK today. In 1313, Bristol and 10 other ports were granted a Statute as "places where English and alien merchants might do business". In 1410 a Charter was granted to hold markets there. By 1500, a society of "Merchant Venturers" was founded and by 1631, Bristol had equal privileges with London for tobacco imports. Around 1700 there was evidence of a growing slave trade but it was short-lived. By 1802, the port was enlarged, to overcome the tides. In 1823, the Bristol Chamber of Commerce was formed and by 1837, the Great Western rail line reached the city. Two years later, the iron founder I. Brunel built the first iron ship nearby. Between 1804 and 1884, the competition with Liverpool became acute and Bristol's three ports were brought in one possession. Finally, by 1908 the port was completely modernized and gained its prime rank as "the port to sail to America from".

Sheffield started as a pig iron producing village, fairly close to a coal mine. It grew into a machinery and miscellaneous manufacturing town. Mining was improved, metals used in construction were added, specially steel "I" beams. The number of iron industrial dealers increased and so did metal goods production. Today, a specialized Steel Patents Library houses no fewer than 25,000 of them, **Sheffield cutlery** has become world famous and even the train from London was called the "Master Cutler Express".

SPECIALIZED FUNCTIONS AND TRAFFIC CONGESTION

Special events leading to the assembly of various functions, tend to create severe traffic congestion and make people and urban planners feel that the city has reached her limits of growth. Further development would be detrimental causing pollution, loss of valuable work time and accidents. Such events and assemblies of functions are:-

International airports; Major shopping parking; World conferences and the protest they give rise to; National Exhibition halls; World Exhibition "Cities"; TV news event coverage; Open air film production; Major pile-up accidents; University and other sports events; even famous personalities entering regional hospitals, may cause congestion.

Computer models of traffic generation by each of the services and functions caused by such assemblies are used to predict trouble spots. A real solution however, would be the dispersal of some functions and at worse, total removal of the less critical facilities. Even more drastic a solution would be to hold conferences and exhibitions at a small village or settlement near the large city.

CITY SIZE AND MAJOR CONFERENCES

A question on Metro size that many Canadians may have asked recently, is :-

WHY hold large meetings (G-8 and G-20 conferences) in megalopolis TORONTO?

- Indeed, a very questionable decision, because any gathering of politicians is likely to discuss controversial matters - and therefore likely to be closely attended by journalists, social media reporters as well as protest groups - all likely to use planes, helicopters, cars, bicycles and buses - to enter an already congested megalopolis.

Traffic movement, accumulation of capital and decision-making activities stimulate urban growth. Why not use this self-evident phenomenon to encourage urban growth in a small municipality? The transfer of personnel (police force, restaurant chefs and waiters, hotel staff, etc) together with appropriate money transfers will stimulate and bring new activities in the small town. If this principle is accepted, all conferences should be held in a little-known towns and hotels, cafes, restaurants, police, etc, would soon follow.

REMEDIAL MEASURES FOR CITIES

Failure of remedial action on traffic congestion in large cities causes out-migration of people to suburbs, but long commuting journeys and lack of service facilities in these suburbs, accounts for the in-migration back to the cities. These problems keep being repeated in many developed countries and there are two remedies:-

(A) **Improve the road network** by dividing the congested city through expensive freeways into a number of equal traffic-generation-zones (Diag. 11). Development control thereafter should ensure that approved proposals for each zone - industrial areas, dense residential estates and traffic-generating new institutions - are more or less balanced between development areas. It would be advisable to allow green space on either side of freeways, to allow for addition of new lanes and for dissipation of traffic noise. A better, long term ecological and social solution would be to relieve the megalopolis of some major functions.

(B) **Dispersion of Service Functions** to existing or new urban districts. Each will have the infrastructure services to satisfy daily and weekly consumer needs, and will also form the service infrastructure for one or two major Function(s) serving the entire city. Diag. 12, (courtesy: Robert Matthew, Johnson-Marshall) shows a distributive road network to provide easier access to the districts and to their special Function(s).

The highly specialized facilities transferred or developed in each district will be selected to suit to the age, or social and economic structure, or cultural characteristics of the local consumer population and develop linkages with infrastructure facilities existing there. Should a district be in development process, the new residents arriving should be given the chance to express their demands through public forum meetings to ensure that the superstructure facilities correspond with the age, socio-economic, income and cultural characteristics of the new district's consumers. Over time and with good teleological planning, each urban district as well as the Centre are likely to develop a distinct sense of place particular to the specialist Function(s) they accommodate.

DEPENDENCE ON USA BORDER CITIES

Listing the reasons for some USA markets attracting Canadians across the border, the main survey findings were as follows:-

USA border city	Reasons for Canadians to visit it
Seattle (Wash)	Seek investor for a software or a computer innovation; Purchasing telecom or computer innovations; Locating a plant in proximity to related industries. City Council open to written development proposals; to high tech industries; High class medical treatment; Seek a computer-related job; Live in highly literate computer- savvy environment.
Great Falls (Mont)	Airport upgrades to Alberta travelers for any USA city Canada Cancer Society support to medical treatment; Birth clinic facilities; Tourism & Recreation research; Avmax Lufthansa transfers from Kabul / Kandahar.
Grand Forks (N. Dak)	Airport use by travelers to any USA city; Banking; Shopping: Macy's, Sears and JC Penney +70 shops in Columbia Mall; 30%-40% discount furniture.
Sault Saint Marie (Min)	Behavioral Health Services; 'AllExperts' medical care (across border) Ben Jovi discography; Variety shopping.
St.Paul's /Minneapolis (Min)	RCMP Operations Training Center for 19 countries; Canadian Consul General; Child diagnostic assessment; Holiday+Tourism; St Paul C Cathedral (St. Peter imitation) Airport; Discount hotels; Galleries; Open air theaters.
Milwakee (Ill)	Airport; Canadian Pacific connection; Recreation; Light industrial products; MRI facilities; Steam train; Museum.
Chicago (Ill)	International Facility Management; Airport control training Child healing environment; 'Agrifood' Biotech cluster Canadian Tourism Commission; Educational events for many professions; Pipeline operation training.
Cleveland (OH)	Airport; PCB storage services; Metal detection;
Port Huron (Mich)	Baker College in rail transport gives accelerated degree courses to Canadians; Rapid freight transport to Quebec City
Detroit (Mich)	Medical treatment; Arts Institute; African history museum
St Catherine's (Mich)	Child medical treatment; Psychology school; Social (across border) work training; Oxford Univ. Press branch.
Bufallo (NY)	Fast USA-Canada immigration permits; Investment; Airport; Electronic exports; Health care; Beginning of Canada-USA industrial corridor; Canadian Airports Council branch; Cheap publishing.

Syracuse (NY)	Medical education; Health services; Manufacturing facilities; Truck-rail + air-rail transfer loads; Storage;.
Rochester (NY)	Airport; Health care; Geriatric services; University; Innovative research on global warming; Car sales; Guest services on Canadian electricity blackouts;
Watertown (NY)	**TV** broadcasting; State-of-the-art medical services; Long stay in discount hotels; Finance; Car sales
Plattsburgh (Vt)	'Allegiant' travel discount line; Passenger service to USA airports; Car sales; Investment; Canada & Quebec university studies; P Postal services; Radio

CONCLUSIONS: Seattle high tech services, cheaper air travel and up-to-date medical services may be difficult to match for quite a number of years, but with advancing recession in USA, many other services could be at least contested, if not surpassed. Detroit's medical function should be the first to be substituted with alternatives in Canada, as that metropolis will continue to decline for some time. Canada should train more doctors as Cuba has done, to earn foreign exchange through medical tourism from USA.

How could this Canadian dependence on USA be reduced? **The answers are fairly obvious:** Higher allocation of funds to **Education**; Develop more jobs for teachers; More medical training for nurses and doctors; Develop Information Technology through more innovations. Produce wind turbine electricity to split water and produce Hydrogen.

DETROIT AND PITTSBURGH - Contrast in dealing with the Recession
Heavily dependent on the manufacture of cars, Detroit suffered very heavy unemployment. Mortgage failures by the thousand, caused a third of the city' homes to fall vacant and houses could be bought for a mere $100.

People went back to cultivating gardens and mini-farming to have vegetables and meat. Capucin Fathers distributed 100,000 plants for people to grow, rather than die of hunger. Richard Florida (1909) forecast that "Detroit will become a ghost town". All sermons and preachers talked about the benefits of charity and that the crisis would take some time to be overcome. Because new technology in developing countries at present and the foreseeable future is likely to be in the field of services and information technology (IT), rather than manufactures.

Pittsburgh, the 'steel town', also suffered heavy unemployment and lost some 800,000 residents due to failed mortgages. But the Council advertised to attract adventure-minded developers to build dense housing (generating chance meetings and ad hoc think-tanks). This was affordable to young computer programmers and Information Technology entrepreneurs.

And the city is growing again…!

Here is an example of creative Council action for Canadian municipalities to bear in mind, in case of the economy receding despite current expectations:-

Encourage ordinary citizens to buy shares in local and Canadian companies with the firm confidence that the economy will stay alive and Canada will overcome the recession suffered by many other countries. The national debt created to stimulate work and carry out the Winter Olympic Games will be soon paid off and the Canadian dollar will continue to stay at almost parity level with USD.

6. CANADA AND THE WORLD BY 2020

WORLD TRENDS AND CANADA'S MARKETS

The number of 'million' cities in the world was 41 in 1945, 83 by 1973 and 264 by 2009. Barring a major catastrophe, urbanization will continue, because even the most noticeable trend of suburbanization, as mentioned earlier, is temporary. All planning authorities are against it. Other noticeable trends:-

Only "developed countries" have small towns and large cities, Canada included; Only the "least developed countries" have few small towns. They face the problem of people looking for employment and a better life, creating growing slums on the periphery of the capital. (McHale, 1953)

Table 4: CANADA'S POPULATION PROJECTIONS 2010-2020 @ 4.5% / ANNUM

2010 = 32.0m	2014 = 38.2m	2018 = 45.5m
2011 = 33.4m	2015 = 39.9m	2019 = 47.6m
2012 = 34.9m	2016 = 41.7m	2020 = 49.7m
2013 = 36.5m	2017 = 43.6m	

By 2031 some 28% of Canada's population will be foreign born and visible minorities of today will have become majorities in Toronto and Vancouver. This is part of the future we accepted by legislating multiculturalism to enhance/diversify Canadian society and develop a stronger economy.

Technology will find new wider development horizons in the technopolis industrial complexes to be developed further in Ottawa (Silicon Valley North), the "technology triangle" - it should now be called 'rectangle' or 'quadrilateral'- of Kitchener-Waterloo-Cambridge-Guelph, Toronto and Vancouver-Seattle.

Garbis Armen, BA, MRTPI, PhD

CANADIAN CITY REGIONS OF LESS THAN 100,000
CURRENT POPULATION LIKELY TO JOIN THE PRESENT ONES IN 2011

In BC:- Dawson Creek   AB: Fort McMurray

SK: Moose Jaw, North Battleford, Prince Albert, Swift Current,

MB: Brandon, Churchill, Flin Flon,   ON: Kenora, Timmins, Trenton, Cobourg.

QC: Joliette, Riviere du Loup, Gaspé   NB: Edmundston, Oromocto, Lancaster

NS: Amherst, Truro.   PEI: Summerside   NL: Corner Brook, Goose Bay.

WHAT NEW FUNCTIONS COULD THE TORONTO MEGALOPOLIS DEVELOP?

Following a study of other megalopolis-size conurbations all over the world, organize a think-tank with sociologists, economists, urban planners, developers, transport engineers and City Hall representatives to set up a few Service Function and traffic network alternatives. These could be discussed at public forums towards selecting a strategy for future development and Service Function structures. Detail plans could thereafter be prepared for districts and local areas to develop local facilities.

GLOBALIZATION

Embodies the diffusion of similar behaviours, processes and systems spreading over the globe. In B. Barber's (1995) book, "JIHAD vs McWORLD: How Globalism and Tribalism are Reshaping the World ", he says that a world defined by technology, culture, communications, capital and consumerism is pitted against fanaticism, parochial hatreds, tribalism and 'ultra-nationalism'. The present era has achieved a level of economic development in which it is possible for innovations occurring in any sector of a country, be instantaneously transferred to and adapted in any other sector or neighbouring country. An innovation accelerates productivity and improves standards of living, and thereafter political and cultural adjustments follow. Robust economic incentives sustain and accelerate the processes of globalization.

SOME FUTURE TECHNOLOGICAL INNOVATIONS

Advanced nanotechnology applied to computers to minimize their volume; Cognitive artificial intelligence; Voice text-ing; Stem cell therapy; Computer resolution of disputes towards World peace; Space tourism; Organ replacement by growing new ones; Human cloning; Privacy under attack; 3-D holography; Biostasis; Cryogenic sleep; Cellular reprogramming; Biotechnology; Instant pain relief; Brain enhancement implants enabling telepathy; Plant genomics ; Biomimetics (Imitating nature - eg. shells - to create novel engineering structures); Weather control; Eco-manipulation; Global warming stability; Megacities; Underground and underwater cities; Smart homes calling 911; Inexpensive genome sequencing; Age reversal; Robotic pets/toys; Cobalt-phosphorus catalyst using electricity to produce hydrogen.

POSSIBLE NOVEL FUNCTIONS

Future power sources and the variety of activities they are likely to generate - from energy conservation to hybrid car production - are sure to give rise to novel Service Functions. Every type of energy - wind, sea tides, solar, geothermal and hydrogen - will generate its own variety of services:-

- Solar design, solar energy consultants, energy engineering professions - and products - like solar panels.

- Wind energy utilization is also quite advanced as to have developed installation engineers, wind turbine repair experts, power transmitter technicians, power assembly stations, etc. Hydrogen (H_2) pressure storage depot; (H_2) utilization consultant, pressure storage cylinder and repair shop, hydrogen car driver school, etc.

- Geothermal heat distribution expert, Geo power home designer, etc.

- Photovoltaic cell panels, PV cell repair shops, roof design and construction.

New requirements will arise for each type of energy - service stations, depots, professionals, repairmen and many new tools will have to be invented.

BENEFITS OF THE SERVICE FUNCTIONS CONCEPT TO THE CITIZEN

What is the relevance of the "city region", "Functions", "propulsive elements" and all that paraphernalia to the day-to-day life of citizens? Here are some ways they could draw a benefit from these ideas -

- On every long journey they make for holidays, they could compare their city region with similar ones and consider gaps in the services or facilities in their own city or town;

- They could form a cultural, entertainment, anti-pollution or any other society they feel could make the voice of the people heard at City Hall. Any such society will be far more effective for the promotion of missing items; They could volunteer for work on missing items or helping in any way they can.

- They could consider prime mover elements - specialized facilities, new leaders, better street lighting and other measures to reduce road accidents, etc – and urge their society to urge the Municipal Council, to promote them. Organize public participation meetings - discussion forums- and protest marches even to the Provincial Legislature or the Federal Parliament.

They should take pride in being creative and effective citizens, dedicated to their city.

7. NOW, SELECT YOUR MARKET

The selection procedure may be summarized as follows:-

(a) Bearing in mind the most likely Age, Occupation, Income and Language of the consumers of your innovative service, product or activity, look at the table of these statistics given for each city region shown in Appendix "C". Select the 4 or 5 most promising city regions for your proposal;

(b) Calculate the Potential Consumer Population for your innovation in each of the selected city regions:-

PCP = Consumer category x Use factor for your service or product. Four Consumer category percentages are given and multiplied with the Population of the city region given on the first line of the page, (next to the city region's name) will give the total clients you could expect from each category. The Use factor for each Consumer category may be selected from Appendix "D"

Consumer category total x Use factor = PCP

(c) Look at the Social and Service Infrastructures in Appendix "A" presented by the existing people, operators and facilities in the market considered bearing in mind that -

System Location Space = Links of functionally associated elements forming service systems at urban or regional or national scales; Linkage values between elements are given in Appendix "D".

Consider the suitability of Geographical features of the area for your innovation, bearing in mind that GEOGRAPHICAL SPACE = Beach, land features, climate, and other characteristics influencing the choice of location for your service outlet.

Ten examples will illustrate the above, referring to Appendices "A" to "D".

EXAMPLES OF INNOVATIONS REACHING THE MARKET

A : The ideal tourist i-phone

A device for person-to-person talk, translation (from English to the language of the country you will visit), text-ing, e-mailing and digital camera.

Best locations to reach relevant consumers:-

International airports by number of flights as follows:-

Toronto, Montreal, Calgary, Vancouver and Halifax.

Soon to follow: Quebec city and Winnipeg.

B: Find markets for the "Zip-Car" car-sharing for convenience.

"Invented" in 1999 in Cambridge Mass,"by a mother of three" (who seems to have copied or plagiarized a German idea). It is a car-sharing-for-profit company, registered as "Zip Car" in 2000 and renting cars by the hour. The HQ was soon moved to Boston and within a few years, some 275,000 drivers driving 6,000 cars in all 49 states had joined.

In 2002, a New York office was opened and in 2005 "Benchmark Capital" provided $10m for expansion. In 2006 it formed a partnership with Satellite Radio and all cars were fitted accordingly. In 2006 established offices first in Toronto, then London, Ontario. In 2007 it merged with Flexcar. In 2009 it was advertised as the largest car-sharing Company. In 2010 the UK branch was established in London (UK) with the name "Streetcar".

<u>Lessons for inventors:</u> ***Move to a large market after forming the company that will apply your invention. Don't hesitate to partner with a company that uses an innovative communication means that will expand your horizons to encompass the entire country; Branching into another country, whether next door or across an ocean, start at the most populous consumer categories for your product.***

C: A lap top computer for the elderly

Considering the "Blackberry" inadequate, an inventor wants to market a small handbag lap-top for elderly, short-sighted, heavy-in-hearing and forgetful people to do shopping calculations, e-mailing and text-ing. Find his markets.

City regions with high "elderly population" profiles in Appendix "C" were as follows:-

Victoria, Kamloops, Sault St. Marie, Thunder Bay, Saskatoon, Winnipeg, Chatham-Kent, Belleville, Saguenay, Granby, St. John (NB), Charlottetown.

Out of these 12 places, he chose Victoria with 137% aged 65+ people above the National average; Kamloops 131%; Sault St Marie 132%; Thunder Bay, 141%; Saskatoon 126%; Winnipeg 138%; Chatham-Kent 121%; Belleville 121% ; Saguenay 134%; Granby 124%; St. John (NB) 134%; and finally Charlottetown 145%;

Rearranging 6 of these which had the highest percentages, the semi-finalists were:- Victoria 137%; Thunder Bay 141%; Sault St. Marie 132%; Saguenay 134%; St John (NB) 134%; and Charlottetown 145%.

Rather than traveling from Victoria (137%), through Thunder Bay (141%); to Charlottetown (145%) he decided it would be wiser to look into the socio-economic percentages as well, before deciding the finalist. Bearing in mind that among the elderly clients he was searching for, ladies would probably be the first to buy his device and they probably used the Clerical skill to earn their living in their younger days, he chose Victoria 119%; Thunder Bay 92% and Charlottetown 90%.

He chose to set up his first retail outlet in Victoria. As there was a large computer store already in that city, he found the manager, signed a brief contract and supplied him with 50 copies of his invention to be sold with the name of his company showing on them. Then he traveled to Kamloops and Thunder Bay.

D: Yet another computer games "gadget" for children 4 - 9 years.

The inventor (or marketing agent), started with Appendix "B" to look for city regions with a high percentage of 0-19 year-olds. The fact that his most likely clients were 4 to 9- year old, could be (a) Dismissed because they would be the same proportion of 0-10 year olds in every city region; or (b) Allowed by dividing each city region's percentage above the National average by 3; or (c) Look into Census 2006 tables for the precise percentage of 4-9 year olds. He solved the problem by adopting course (a).

Looking into Appendix "C" he listed the following:- Barrie-Orillia, Red Deer, Lethbridge, Montreal, Sarnia, Kawartha Lakes, London and Niagara Falls.

Checking on the percentages above the National average in Appendix "C", he came up with:- Red Deer 107%; Lethbridge 108%; Montreal 110%; Sarnia 120%; Kawartha Lakes 115%; London 109%; Barrie-Orillia 128%; Niagara Falls 120%;

Arranging these in descending order he ended with Barrie-Orillia, Niagara Falls, Sarnia, Kawartha Lakes, Montreal, Lethbridge and Red Deer as the most promising "youngster" markets and he set up the first retail store in the booming new city of Barrie-Orillia (18%+ growth in 2001-2006). In large cities - Montreal – which had their long existing computer stores, he signed a consignment agreement with their managers and left them a supply to sell.

E : Find the market for an anti-pollution home-air-cleaning device

Such a useful innovation for many polluted cities all over the world, could best be first- marketed in Canada's heavily polluted city of Sudbury - shown on Map 4 of Appendix "B". None of the population statistics shown against that city region's age and s/e profile need be studied in this case, because the device would meet the needs of all people, but especially asthma suffering elderly persons.

The inventor would rent an office or retail store in downtown Sudbury, place large posters and detail description of his invention and have a young, white-dressed man and woman, demonstrating the device. In case of willing home owners wishing to see a demonstration in their home, this should be encouraged and rewarded. In due course, two or three outlets in Sudbury's hinterland would be established and Province-wide adverts on TV would ensure good publicity of the invention to make its mass-production economically viable.

Lesson for inventors: ***Start diffusing the device at the place of greatest need for it.***

There are also six sources of natural pollution to guard against: - (1) The greenhouse effect due to sunshine and methane; (2) Acid rain; (3) Particulate contamination; (4) Ultra-violate radiation; (5) Increased Ozone concentration; (6) Increased Nitrogen.

F : The ultra-modern hairdresser saloon.

The Acadian grandfather of a young lady, graduate of a Swiss Finishing School, decided to present her a luxurious hairdressing saloon as a graduation present. Should he set up the saloon in her hometown or venture elsewhere?

She took her grandfather to the office of a market consultant to ask for advice. The consultant had a copy of "Prime Markets in Canada" and started with Appendix "B" to find city regions which had an above-National average percentage of prosperous females likely to afford visiting the projected luxury saloon. He sieved them further by looking up Appendix "C" as to ages 20-24 and 25-64 and went to a third sieve of Socio-economic percentages, by assuming that the Clerical profession was their most likely occupation in their younger days. He ended up with the following list of semi-finalists:- Montreal, Toronto, London (ON), Calgary and Lethbridge.

Calgary among these had the highest family income $118,000. Pure sentiment, however, made her also add her hometown: Charlottetown city region. She now asked for all the figures to show her grandfather.

The Income, Age and Socio-economic percentages of the semi-finalist city regions, as shown in Appendix "C" were: - Calgary 108%, 128%, 117%; Lethbridge 108%,109%, 107%; London (ON) 109%, 122%, 104%; Montreal 110%, 123%, 121%; Toronto 113%, 125%, 120%; Charlottetown 87%, 93%, 90%.

When the consultant presented the above figures to them, they realized that Charlottetown was not the best candidate city region for the luxury saloon they had in mind. Toronto was the most promising, but competition there was likely to be tough. Montreal was second best, Calgary third and London (ON) fourth.

The Acadian young lady spoke Swiss French and fashionable Montreal was nearer to her hometown - and her heart. She opened the luxury saloon in that metropolis.

G: Where should a quality restaurant go?

A Greek immigrant started a restaurant in Toronto's "Greektown" and after years of entire family effort, he got rich and ambitious and wanted to promote himself to a "Quality Restaurateur". He ordered a realtor to find larger, more prestigious premises.

After months of looking at "Greektown" locations, the realtor took him to see a restaurant within view of the Toronto Stock Exchange. The lease was quite expensive. He bought a copy of "Prime Markets in Canada" and after reading about "System location" in Sections 3 and 4, he knew straight away that any location within sight of the Stock Exchange would bring prestige to his quality restaurant.

Departing from "Greektown" however, would not be easy. He and his wife would lose many friendships and the children would be too far from the Greek school. They could still go to Sunday church Orthodox service and on March 25 "Greek Independence" celebrations, they could still join the parade behind the huge blue-and-white, street-wide flag. But some patriotic sentiment would be lost in the children.

He decided to move his business near the Stock Exchange, keep his "Greektown" home and commute to Toronto Centre to manage the restaurant. He forgot the habit of asking the family to peel potatoes and cook meals every day, and engaged bow-tied staff to service his well-to-do clients.

H. The learning robot

A Japanese inventor perfected the robotic science dream of a domestic housework-learning-robot. It could view a task performed by a lady, convert it into an action program and repeat it, by association with a command. The inventor aimed to sell it to rich housewives in the largest cities and he would like to start in west USA and after reaching New York, 'jump' the Atlantic and continue selling it in Europe.

How about Canada?

After demonstrating the robot's capabilities in Los Angeles, he sent an agent to Vancouver. Advertising on CBC TV with a demonstration, the agent sold a good number in the "British Properties" area of the city. The inventor agreed that a service outlet should be set up in that city and the agent should move to other Canadian cities. On what criteria should he base his choice?

On the basis of a 10% sample of the earliest buyers of the robot, he decided that over-65-aged ladies from Professional / Managerial homes with an $80k+ family Income were the most likely buyers. He decided to look into the "Prime Markets in Canada" guide and found that Calgary (72% of age 65+; 132% of Manag. / Prof.; 52% of $80k+ highest family income at $118,000 / annum; and 79% Anglophone population - comparing with the National average) should be the second city to see and buy the robot.

Next was Edmonton's turn (87%; 129%; 9%; 78%) and in "West Edmonton Mall" he sold quite a few. Regina (87%; 139%; 3%; 58%) was next, followed by Saskatoon (126%; 111%; 5%; 54%), Winnipeg (138%; 120%; 4%; 49%), Toronto (72%; 138%; 45%; 51%) and Ottawa-Gatineau (102%; 141%; 12%; 29%) The agent now engaged a Francophone salesman and they ventured into Quebec. In Montreal (89%; 106%; 31%; 69% Francophone) and Quebec city (87%; 138%; 14%; 78% Francophone) they shared the work on the markets, while in Halifax (123%; 121%; 6%; 79% English) it was the English speaking agent that took over the task of showing the computer). Here, the inventor instructed them to set up regional distribution outlets in each Province and report the fastest selling city regions, so as to judge his invention's rate of diffusion and decide the second and third wave of outlets.

Thereafter he signed agreements with Canadian companies in smaller cities or large city suburbs, to ensure country-wide diffusion of his robot. At that point he ordered mass-production and lowered the price of the robot to ensure that even in villages, rich elderly housewives bought that robot.

J. The ultimate educator

An education "expert" compiled a bilingual DVD which could teach all school subjects on a lap-top computer allowing each student to advance at his own pace. This anti-social device was not popular with schools. Where should he start from?

After advertising on TV to gather negative as well as some positive comments, he listed all city regions with large proportions of 3-19 year olds and went to their largest bookshops to offer his DVD. The city regions were:-

Barrie-Orillia (128%); Calgary (108%); Kawartha Lakes (115%); Kingston (121%); Lethbridge (108%); London (ON) (109%); Montreal (110%); Niagara Falls (120%), North Bay (106%); Ottawa-Gatineau (108%); Red Deer (107%); Sarnia (120%); St. Hyacynthe (110%); Toronto (113%); Windsor (102%).

Out of 15 candidate city regions, he chose the upper 7:- Barrie-Orillia, Kawartha Lakes, Kingston, Montreal, Niagara Falls, Sarnia, Windsor and Toronto to be the prime distribution outlets. He signed consignment contracts.

He received some protest letters, but knowing that none could result in court action, he remained indifferent and continued his "important educational mission" to adults who, for various reasons, had not graduated from any school.

K: Find the market for a floating restaurant innovation.

In the "Vancouver Sun" of July 8th 2010, Mia Stainsby had an article about the opening of a 12-seat restaurant floating on 1,700 plastic bottles, offering for a multi-course seafood meal for 60 days to collect funds for a non-profit School of the FishFoundation. The inventor was the School's founder, Shannon Ronalds who wanted to "help save the world's remaining fish."

He had the brainwave of such a restaurant while pressed by a sense of urgency to organize an event only 13 days away. "The engineering challenge was to make sure the thing wouldn't flip over and sink." Above the 1,700 bottles there is the restaurant's wooden floor with transparent Plexiglass inserts to allow diners to view the assembled bottles below them.

Some 720 people dining over 60 days enjoyed the exceptional experience. All other clients visiting and dining thereafter established Fish Foundation restaurant as a permanent facility, increasing the number of tables and turnover month after month.

<u>Lessons for inventors:</u> ***Plant an invention in its natural setting to attract concerned people to your cause (Restaurant; seaside; large fish-eating city). Ally your marketing of the invention to a charity close to the heart of the people of that city. If the cause is to save fish, feed your clients other seafood - crabs, etc - but not fish.***

EPILOGUE

Canada has bright prospects for further social and economic growth, by reason of the growing human capital, freedom from serious threats from global warming, plentiful physical resources and natural beauty. All the markets mentioned here are certain to grow and the most important reasons are worth reiterating.

The human capital of this great country is to be found in the continuing "open doors" immigration policy, the inventiveness of new and born-Canadians and the venturesome spirit present in all of them. The "open doors" policy is Canada's way to help the poor people and countries of the world - lending a helping hand to their technology and prospects.

Global warming may cause some flooding of Canada's ports and coastline, but the melting of ice and receding glacial areas will allow for the expansion of habitable areas through the inventive use of glass for solar heat gain, transparent plastic and geodesic structures to cover large areas - particularly downtown market areas - and other climate control inventions yet to come.

The great variety of mineral resources and the endless forests of Canada have been the mainstay of the country's economy for four centuries now, but they are increasingly giving way to services and Information Technology in particular. Marketing innovations may be only expected to grow therefore and entrepreneurs wise enough to create new markets in this promising land, can only stand to gain.

REFERENCES

Alexander, C: (1966): A City is not a Tree, pp.46-55; DESIGN # 206, Feb,1966.

Armen, G. (1971): Service Functions & Urban Character : A systems approach to the growth and distribution of services with application to the planning of new communities (PhD thesis mimeographed by the Dept. of the Environment, UK)

Armen, G. (1972): A Classification of Cities and City Regions in England & Wales, 1966 Regional Studies, Vol 6. No 2 pp 149-182 Pergamon Press UK)

Armen, G. (1975) : The growth of ethnic markets in Canadian cities. (Chinese seminar lecture)

Barber, B: (1995): Jihad Vs Mc World (Ballantine, NY)

Barnet, N: (1996): The State of the Cybernation. (London, UK)

Berry BJL, Garrison, (1958): Functional Bases of the Central Place Hierarchy. Economic Geography, No. 34

Burton, I: (1963): A Restatement of the Dispersed City Hypothesis. (Annals of the Assoc'n of American Geographers, No 53)

Beaujot R & Kerr D : (2007) Changing Face of Canada (Canadian Scholars Press, Ottawa.).

Christaller. W: (1933) : Central Places in Southern Germany (translated by C. W. Baskin) Prentice Hall (1966)

Florida, R : (2009) : How will the crush reshape America. "Atlantis" Feb. 2009 issue.

Geddes, P : (1915): Cities in Evolution. Republished 1949, 1968 (London).

Green, FHW: (1950): Urban Hinterlands of England and Wales, Geogr'cal Journal, CXVI.

Green, F.H.W. : (1956): Community of Interest Areas. Economic Geography #34.

Hall, P. G.; Castells, M. (1994): Technopoles of the World. Routledge, (London UK)

Jones, E : (1966): Towns and Ciities (Oxford University Press) London

Kuene, R.E. (1968) : Microscopic Theory of the Market Mechanism: A general equilibrium approach (Collier-Macmillan, pp 10-24 NY)

Golledge, R.G. (1967): Conceptualizing the Market Decision Process. Journal of Reg. Science & (2)

Jones, E: (1966) : Human Geography (London, UK)

Machiavelli, N: (1531) : Discourse on the First Decade of Titus Livius (London, UK)

Mc Hale, (1974) : Future World Trends and Alternative Futures (NY)

Ministry of Transport (1970) : Bus Routes and Hinterlands. (London, UK)

von Netterdorf, A (1809) : Die Elemente Der Statskunte (Berlin)

Ng, RCY: (1969): Recent Internal Movement in Thailand (London, UK)

Popper, KR. (1958) : The Logic of Scientific Discovery. Hutchinsons (London, UK)

Porter,J (1965): The Vertical Mosaic: Analysis of Social Class & Power in Canada (Toronto)

Ratcliff, RU.: (1955): The Dynamics of Efficiency in the Distribution of Urban Activities. (Readings in Urban Geography)

Rannells, J. (1956) : The Core of the City (Philadelphia)

Scott A.J. (1968) : Functional & Spatial structure of the central city: A mathematical theory and an empirical test. Discussion Paper, Graduate Sch. of Geography, L. Sc. of Economics.

Thomas, J. (1968) : A Queueing Theory analogue for scree slope studies.(London, UK)

Trembay, A : (1956) Quelques Aspects de notre Proble'me Scolaire (Quebec)

Turgot, A. (1844): Reflexions sur la Formation et la Distribution des Richesses (Paris)

Useful websites:

1. Statistics Canada (2009) http://www.stacan.gc.ca / daily

2. Statistics Canada (2006) Www40.stat.ca/101/demo 05a-eng htm

3. http://www12.statcan.ca/english/census06/data/topics/RetrieveProductTable.cfm?

4. Http://en.wikipedia.org/wiki/Demographics_of_Canada

THE SERVICE FUNCTIONS

The following 10 pages give the definition of Service Functions in terms of -

A. Range and specialization level of services / facilities / institutions and voluntary associations / societies that had developed in Canada by 2006

B. The Social Infrastructure required in terms of operators (managers, chefs, waiters and personnel in general) and consumers distinguished in two socio-economic and age groups;

C. The Service Infrastructure linkages between the facilities / services at the top layers of the Function - the Superstructure

D. Suggested distance between facilities which should preferably be located within walking distance of each other, to bring convenience and a sense of place / identity to a group / neighborhood centre.

The top four layers forming the Superstructure of a Function show the Specialized services / facilities which require above 80,000 population in a city to be viable. If PCP calculations based on socio-economic and age data show a high number of consumers and public participation meetings / forums indicate a strong desire for any Specialized activity - a music enthusiast community for example - starting with occasional / trial performances the service / activity could be provided until the desired facility is built.

A word of caution about developers of large housing estates, building "high class" facilities - golf course, opera, concert hall etc - even before homes have been completed, as a promotional device to sell homes to wealthy clients (Armen, 1971). Sociologists consider this a form of "**social engineering**". A Specialized facility should be called for by the **people,** promoted by a **society** they have formed, provided by that society with an **entrance ticket to pay** and finally built with **public collection as well as Federal and Provincial** funds.

This is the reason for Diagram 06 being called "A **Social** Development Model".

A D M I N I S T R A T I O N

Million +	**SUPERSTRUCTURE**	Federal Ministry; International airport;
500-M		Consulate; Courts; Local radio station; 5-star hotel
250-499		Provincial ministry; County Administration
80-249		Reference library; Business/Trade Association; Quality restaurant; City Hall.

25-79.9	**INFRASTRUCTURE**	Fire station; Magistrate's court; 3-star hotel; Motel; Hospital; Post office; Local newspaper; Municipal offices; Cultural society; Monument; Rail station, Political org's
10-24.9		Police station; Political clubs; Public library; Hockey pitch; Clinic; Rooming House; Shopping mall; Community centre; Recreational society; Post office; Labour exchange.
1-9,9		Restaurant; Social club; Post office; Children's play area; Public house; Café/Snack bar; Assembly hall; Day care; Church; Welfare/Religious society; Social club.

Average catchment (000-s popl'n) as a proxy scale of specialization of an activity

SOCIAL INFRASTRUCTURE:	1	2	3	4
Age group % :	30.9	6.8	49.8	12.5
S/E group % :	15.4	39.5	21.0	24.1

SERVICE INFRASTRUCTURE:

Federal Ministry-Internat'nal airport = 685   Cultural society-Monument = 598
Provinc'l ministry-County Administr'n = 691   Shops-Commun'ty centre = 765
Reference library-Business/Trade Association = 702
Local newspaper-Municipal offices = 645   Quality restaurant-City Hall = 587

FACILITIES LINKED BY PEDESTRIAN WALK

Day care-Church-Welfare/Religious society   Magistrate's court- 3-star hotel
Motel-café/snack bar-Shops-Commun'ty centre
Café/Snack bar-Assembly hall;   Public library-Hockey pitch
Rooming House-Shopping mall-Pub   Children's play area-Day care

HEALTH & WELFARE

Million +	Regional hospital (Teaching surgery, MRI use, etc); University
500-M	Mental Hospital
250-499	Pharmacy; Supermarkets; County Administration.
80-249	Provincial ministry; Reference library; Quality restaurant; Airport;
25-79.9	Hospital; Museum; 3-star hotel; Motel; Local newspaper; Local authority offices ; Cinema
10- 24.9	Health centre; Public library; Welfare society; Clinic; Rail station; Cultural society; Recreational society; Post office; Restaurant
01-9,9	Sports club; Post office; Pub; Social club; Religious society Children's playground; Day care; Pl. of worship; Café/Snack bar. Preschool.

SOCIAL INFRASTRUCTURE

	Emp/Prof	Clerical	Skilled	Indefinite
S/E group % :	20.0	32.5	18.3	29.2
	Youth	Swing	Parents	Retired
Age group % :	32.4.	6.3	48.1	13.2

SERVICE INFRASTRUCTURE Values of main linkages
Regional hospital-Pharmacy = 675   Reg. Hosp-Ref Liby = 762
Health centre-Welfare soc. = 492   Pub-Social club = 764

FACILITIES LINKED BY PEDESTRIAN WALK
University, Regional Hospital   Airport-Restaurants-Café/Snack bars
Libraries-Schools-Day care, Post office, Clubs, Shops-Bus / Train / Skytrain

E D U C A T I O N

Million +	Regional hospital (Teaching surgery, MRI use, etc)
500-M	University; Polytechnic; 5-star hotel
250-499	Specialized college (Art, Design, Tech, etc); Sports hall; Teachers' Training College; Theatre,; County Administration
80-249	Reference library; Stadium; Business/Trade Association; Provincial ministry branch; Quality restaurant; Airport; Cinema.
25-79.9	Further educ. college; Museum; Gallery; 3-star hotel; Motel; Swimming pool; Local newspaper; Local authority offices.
10- 24.9	Secondary sch; Public library; Hockey pitch; Clinic; Rail station; Cultural society; Recreational society; Post office. Secondary school
1-9,9	Restaurant; Sports club; Post office; Pub; Social club; Children's playground; Day care; Church; Café/Snack bar. Welfare/Religious society; Preschool; Primary School

Average catchment (000-s popl'n) as a proxy scale of specialization of an activity

SOCIAL INFRASTRUCTURE:	1	2	3	4
Age group % :	34.2	12.0	47.3	6.5
S/E group % :	16.2	39.6	18.3	28.9

SERVICE   INFRASTRUCTURE

University-Stadium = 743   University-Sports hall = 738   Stadium-Pub = 762
Polytechnic-Univ'ty = 469   Botanical gardens-Recreational society = 513
Specialized college-Ref Liby = 689

FACILITIES LINKED BY PEDESTRIAN WALK

University-Polytechnic-College departments   Theatre-Restaurants
Café/Snack bars-Sports club   Restaurant-Sports club-Pub
Library-Schools   Day care-Café   Clubs-Shops-Bus / Train / Skytrain

PHYSICAL   RECREATION

Million +	University; TV studio; Radio station; Olympic swimming pool
500-M	Sports hall; Bowling alley; 5-star hotel; Zoo; Sports hall; Airport.;
250-499	Stadium; Supermarket; Gliding/Flying base/Sailing club. Quality restaurant; Wrestling; Holiday camp; Greyhound racing.
80-249	Dancing hall; Swimming (indoor/outdoor pools); Boating base; Quality restaurant; 18-hole golf course
25-79.9	Swimming pool; 3-star hotel; Park; Further Educ. College; Hockey arena; Yachting club; Holiday camp; Golf course; Race track,, Stadium; Bike path.
10- 24.9	Shopping area; Cultural society; Recreational society; Inn Political clubs; Restaurant; Public library; Camping site. Cine/Bingo; Bowling green; Hockey arena; Night club; Motel.
01-9,9	Recrn'l/Social club; Post office; Pub; Children's play area; Religious/Welfare society; Pl. of worship; Social club; Meeting room; Clinic; Football pitch; Primary school; Park; Boarding house; Tennis court; Children's play area; Cafe

SOCIAL INFRASTRUCTURE

	Emp/Prof	Clerical	Skilled	Indefinite
S/E group % :	15.3	40.0	14.8	29.9
	Youth	Swing	Parents	Retired
Age group % :	32.5	7.5	48.0	12.0

SERVICE INFRASTRUCTURE Value of main linkages

Olympic swimming pool-Sports hall = 804   Dance hall-Quality Rest'nt = 789
Holiday camp-Bike path = 668   Tennis court-Café = 764
5-star hotel-Supermarket = 654   Wresling-Sports hall = 698

FACILITIES LINKED BY PEDESTRIAN WALK

University - Swimming pool - Café   Zoo - Restaurant - Pub   Tennis ct - cafe
Dance hall - Quality Restaurant   Olympic swimming pool - Sports hall - cafe
Restaurant - Café/Snack bars   Social club - Meeting room - pub - Cafe

HOLIDAY   RESORT   FUNCTION

Million +	Variety theatre; Concert hall; Casino; TV studio; Radio station;
500-M	Zoological garden; Bowling alley; 5-star hotel; Airport;
250-499	Theatre; Gliding/Flying base; Sailing club; Army & Navy; Zellers;
80-249	Dancing hall; Beauty contests; Greyhound racing; Swimming; Boating base; Quality restaurant; Airport.; 18-hole golf course
25-79.9	Museum; Gallery; Theatrical activity / club; 3-star hotel; Local newspaper; Yachting club; Holiday camp; Fire station Retirement homes; Sportsfishing club; Amusement park, Botanical gdns; Marina; Undersea gdns; 9-hole golf course
10- 24.9	Shopping area; Cultural society; Recreational society; Political clubs; Restaurant; Public library; Camping site; Cine/Bingo; Bowling green; Hockey arena; Night clubs; Bike path, Campground; Motels; Caravan sites
01-9,9	Restaurant; Social club; Post office; Pub; Children's play area; Relig/Welf society; Pl of worship; Social club; Meeting room. Clinic; Football pitch; Boarding house; Park; Camping site; Tennis court; Entertainment club; Cafe/Snack

SOCIAL INFRASTRUCTURE

	Emp/Prof	Clerical	Skilled	Indefinite
S/E group % :	19.4	33.6	19.8	27.2

	Youth	Swing	Parents	Retired
Age group % :	23.7	6.6	48.4	21.3

SERVICE INFRASTRUCTURE   Value of main linkages
Boating-Camping site = 568   Yachting club-Holiday camp-Cafe
Hotel-Bus stop = 764 Pl. of Worship-Welfare society = 698

FACILITIES LINKED BY PEDESTRIAN WALK
Theatre - Restaurants - Cafes; Post office - Clubs;   Café - Clubs / Societies;
Libraries - Schools - Day care- Shops   Shops-Bus / Train / Skytrain;
Hotel - Airport - Train station   Motel - restaurant - Social club

E N T E R T A I N M E N T

Million +	Variety theatre; Casino; TV studio; Radio station ; First-run-cinema

---

500-M	Bowling alley; 5-star hotel; Horse racing

250-499	(Comedy) theatre, Port / Harbour

80-249	Dance hall; Beauty contests; Greyhound racing; Quality restaurant; Airport.;

25-79.9	Cinema; Night club; 3-star hotel; Local newspaper; Computer store

---

10- 24.9	Shopping area; Jewelers; Army and Navy; Wal-Mart; Zellers; Restaurant; Police station; Shopping mall; 2-star hotel; Motel; Cine/Bingo; Night club; Betting shop; Harbour.

01-9,9	Restaurant; Social club; Post office; Pub; Social club; Children's playground; Religious/Welfare society; Church; Meeting room, Clinic; Welfare soc; Football pitch; Boarding house; Public house; Park; Camping site; Tennis court; Entertainment club; Cafe/Snack

SOCIAL INFRASTRUCTURE

	Emp/Prof	Clerical	Skilled	Indefinite
S/E group % :	3.6	45.0	16.5	32.9
	Youth	Swing	Parents	Retired
Age group % :	32.0	7.4	47.7	12.9

SERVICE INFRASTRUCTURE Value of main linkages

Casino-5 star hotel = 764   Dance hall-First run cinema = 686
Computer store - Shopping area = 769   Wal-mart - café = 754
Dance hall - Beauty contests = 832   Airport - Cinema = 748
Casino - Quality rest'nt = 698   Theatre - Quality rest'nt = 767

FACILITIES LINKED BY PEDESTRIAN WALK

Casino - Quality restaurant;   Theatre - Restaurants - Café/Snack bars
Library - Schools, Post office - Clubs - Shops - Bus / Train / Skytrain

P O R T   F U N C T I O N

Million +	Consulate; Casino; Radio station, Variety theatre, TV studio
500-M	5-star hotel; Horse racing; Bowling alley
250-499	Port. or harbour, Dancing hall.
80-249	Dancing hall; Greyhound racing; Quality restaurant; Airport;
25-79.9	Cinema; Night club; 3-star hotel; Local newspaper; Zellers.
10- 24.9	Shopping area; Jewelers; Army and Navy; Wal-Mart; Doctors; Restaurant; Police station; Shopping mall; 2-star hotel; Motel; Bingo hall; Betting shop; Harbour.
01-9,9	Restaurant; Post office; Pub; Movers; Social club; Meeting room; Welfare society; Boarding house; Public house. Park; Entertainment club; Cafe/Snack

SOCIAL INFRASTRUCTURE

	Emp/Prof	Clerical	Skilled	Indefinite
S/E group % :	12.1	41.0	15.0	31.9
	Youth	Swing	Parents	Retired
Age group % :	33.0	6.2	48.1	12.7

SERVICE INFRASTRUCTURE Value of main linkages

Consulate - Port = 765   Variety theatre - Quality restaurant = 767
Casino - Restaurant = 776   Dance hall - Quality restaurant = 789   Dance hall - café = 762
Greyhound racing - restaurant = 758   Shopping area - Jewelers = 734
Bingo hall - Entertainment club = 698   Zellers - Shopping area = 756
Port - Shopping area = 769   Airport - shops = 754

FACILITIES LINKED BY PEDESTRIAN WALK

Shops-Betting shop-Cinema-Pub   Airport-Qual rest'nt-Meeting room
Restaurant-Café/Snack   Theatre-Restaurants-Café/Snack bars
Libraries-Post office   Clubs-Shops-Bus / Train / Skytrain

S P E C I A L I Z E D   S H O P P I N G

Million +	Sears; The Bay; TV station.
500-M	5-star hotel; Wine Institute.
250-499	Office area; County administration; Retirement home; Wal-Mart
80-249	Police station; Community centre ; Rail station; Town hall; Quality restaurant; Airport; Army & Navy; Zellers; Market, Wineries.
25-79.9	Fire station; Night club; 3-star hotel; Local newspaper; Cinema.
10- 24.9	Shopping mall; Jewelers; Army and Navy; Wal-Mart; Doctors; Restaurant; 2-star hotel; Motel; Computer store; Public library Bingo hall; Betting shop. Computer store, Video sales
01-9,9	Restaurant; Post office; Pub; Movers; Social club; Meeting room; Welfare society; Boarding house; Public house. Dollar store. Park; Entertainment club; Café/Snack; Play area; Retail shops.

SOCIAL INFRASTRUCTURE

	Emp/Prof	Clerical	Skilled	Indefinite
S/E group % :	14.4	42.0	18.3	25.3
	Youth	Swing	Parents	Retired
Age group % :	29.1	6.8	48.2	15.9

SERVICE INFRASTRUCTURE   Value of main linkages

Sears - Army & Navy = 658   Wine institute - Wineries = 835
Police station-Local newspaper = 736 Fire station - Hotels = 590
5-star hotel - Market = 573   Retirement home - Sears = 694
Office area - The Bay = 785   Shopping mall - Wineries = 743

FACILITIES LINKED BY PEDESTRIAN WALK

Shopping mall-Bus stops-Skytrain   Computer store-Shopping mal-cafe
Restaurants-Shopping mall-Café/Snack bars   Day care-Shops, Post office, Clubs,
Shops-Bus stop-Skytrain   Police station-Shopping mall-Boarding house

BUSINESS & PROFESSIONAL SERVICES

Million +	Stock Exchange; International airport; TV station; Federal offices.
500-M	5-star hotel; Consulate; Customs & Excise; Bankruptcy court.
250-499	Office area; Law courts; County administration; Jewelers; Hotels. Federal business ass'ce centre; Business consultant;
80-249	Police station; Reference library ; Rail station; Town hall; Quality restaurant; Airport; Zellers; Market; Trade associations
25-79.9	Fire station; Night club; 3-star hotel; Local newspaper; Cinema.
10- 24.9	Shopping mall; Jewelers; Army and Navy; Wal-Mart; Train station; Restaurant; 2-star hotel; Motel; Computer store; Public library Bingo hall; Political club; Investment advisor; Employment agency
01-9,9	Restaurant; Post office; Pub; Social club; Meeting room; Welfare society; Public house. Cultural society; Family doctor; Park; Entertainment club; Café/Snack;

SOCIAL INFRASTRUCTURE

	Emp/Prof	Clerical	Skilled	Indefinite
S/E group % :	15.4	40.5	18.8	26.3
	Youth	Swing	Parents	Retired
Age group % :	31.5	6.9	50.1	11.5

SERVICE INFRASTRUCTURE Value of main linkages

Stock exchange-International airport = 732   Federal offices-Bankruptcy ct = 784
5-star hotel-Business consultants = 688   Shopping mall-Jewelers = 763
Army & Navy- Wal-Mart = 659   Zellers-Market = 657
Federal business ass'ce centre-Train station = 676 Dollar store-Café/Snack = 761

FACILITIES LINKED BY PEDESTRIAN WALK

Stock exchange-Quality restaurant   Federal offices-Bankruptcy ct-Cafe
5-star hotel-Business consultant offices   Shopping mall-Jewelers-Restaurant
Army & Navy- Wal-Mart-Zellers-Market   Pub-Bus / Skytrain-Shopping mall
Stock Exchange-Federal offices-Office area   Employment agency-Business
Restaurant-2-star hotel-Motel-Pub-Social club-Meeting room

M E T R O   C I T Y   S E R V I C E S

Million +	Stock Exchange; International airport; TV studio; Federal offices.
500-M	5-star hotel; Embassy, University; Colleges; Sears; The Bay; Hospital
250-499	Office area; Army & Navy; Wal-Mart; Jewellers; Zellers; 4-star hotels Business consultant. Specialized colleges; Sports hall; Hospital;
80-249	Police station; Reference library ; Rail station; Town hall; Port; Quality restaurant; Airport; Zellers; Market; Trade associations
25-79.9	Special library; Night club; 3-star hotels; Local newspaper; Cinema; Night club; Gliding base; Courts; Office area; Stadium; Prov ministry
10- 24.9	Shopping mall; Health centre; Political clubs; Welfare societies Restaurant; 2-star hotel; Computer store; Public library Shopping mall; Train station; Computer store; Video store;
01-9,9	Restaurant; Post office; Pub; Social club; Meeting room; Clinic; Welfare society; Public house. Cultural society; Park; Café/Snack; Betting shop; Café/Snack ; Retail shops; Dollar store; Social club.

SOCIAL INFRASTRUCTURE

	Emp/Prof	Clerical	Skilled	Indefinite
S/E group % :	14.6	39.4	18.0	28.0
	Youth	Swing	Parents	Retired
Age group % :	32.7	7.7	49.3	10.3

SERVICE INFRASTRUCTURE   Value of main linkages

5-star hotel-Business consultant offices = 684   Shopping mall-Jewelers = 786
Restaurant - Army & Navy = 587   Wal-Mart-Zellers-Market = 681
Business consltant-Federal business ass'ce centre = 769
Skytrain-Federal offices = 683   Stock Exchange-Federal office = 723

FACILITIES LINKED BY PEDESTRIAN WALK

Shops, Bus / Train / Skytrain - café - Restaurants   2-star hotel-Café/Snack bar
Stock Exchange-Federal offices-Office area   Motel-Pub-Social club-Meeting room
5-star hotel-Business consltant-Federal business ass'ce centre-Train station
Shopping mall-Jewelers-Army & Navy-Wal-Mart-Zellers-Market-Café/Snack;

The following six pages present the selected 49 city regions as communities with individual age and socio-economic characteristics in their **regional context,** as follows:-

- The **thick-lined square** and the number under it indicate the **market's relative population size;**

- The **four columns on the left,** represent the relative proportions of four **Age groups,** in comparison with the **National Average of these groups, shown as a horizontal line;**

- The **four columns on the right,** represent the relative proportions of four **S/e groups,** always in comparison with the **National Average,** shown as a continuation of the line of the Average for age groups.

- These **eight statistics,** together with **another eight for Income and Language** are shown as percentages above or below the National Average, implied with the figure of 100%, below city region maps on Appendix "C". This 100% is also implied by the above-mentioned horizontal line on every city region's profile, in Appendix "B"..

- The **shaded circle** and city name show the **geographical location** of the market in its **regional context** to imply the potential for the **development of links between markets.**

This potential may be realized by any means of current and future technological **communication or physical transportation,** from fax and e-mail to rail and jet plane, carrying CEO's for important meetings.

COMPARISON OF PRIME MARKETS:
BY AGE & SOCIO-ECONOMIC STRUCTURE OF CATCHMENT

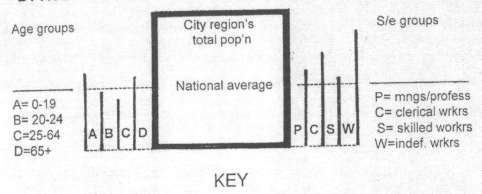

Age groups

City region's
total pop'n

National average

S/e groups

A= 0-19
B= 20-24
C=25-64
D=65+

A B C D

P C S W

P= mngs/profess
C= clerical wrkrs
S= skilled workrs
W=indef. wrkrs

KEY

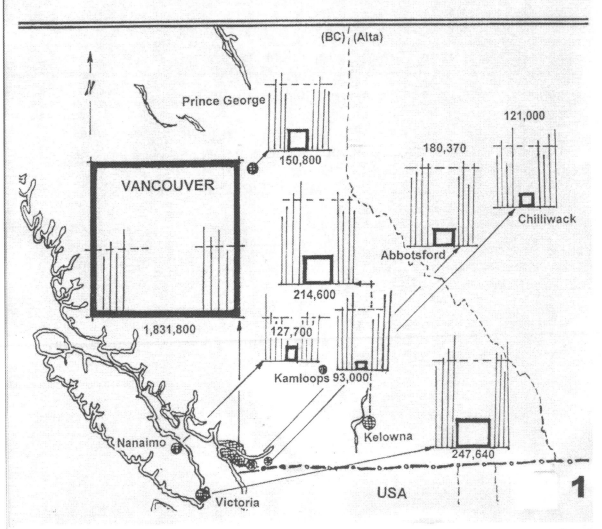

(BC) (Alta)

Prince George

121,000

150,800

180,370

VANCOUVER

Chilliwack

Abbotsford

214,600

1,831,800

127,700

Kamloops 93,000

Kelowna

Nanaimo

247,640

Victoria

USA

1

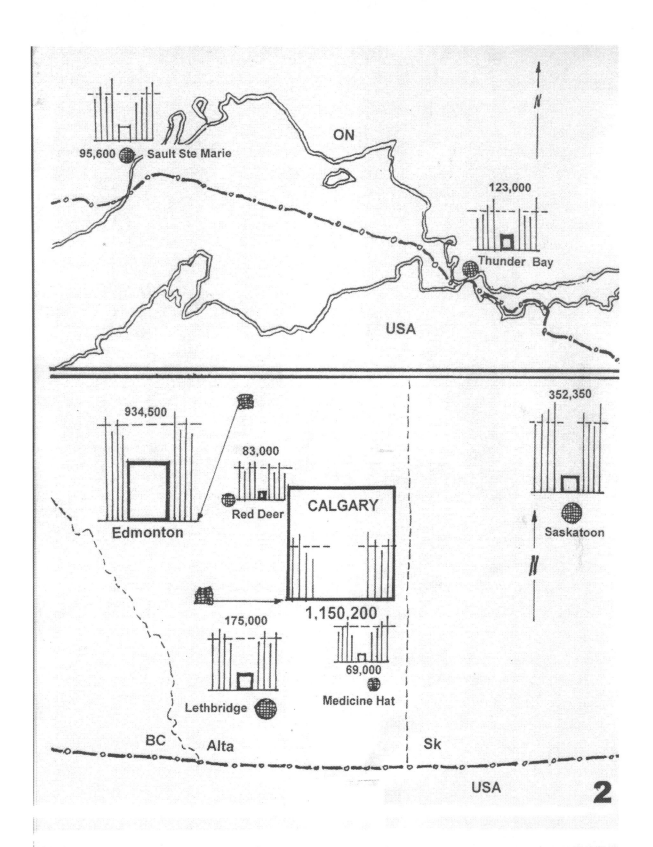

95,600 Sault Ste Marie

ON

123,000 Thunder Bay

USA

934,500 Edmonton

83,000 Red Deer

CALGARY

1,150,200

352,350 Saskatoon

175,000 Lethbridge

69,000 Medicine Hat

BC   Alta   Sk

USA

2

71

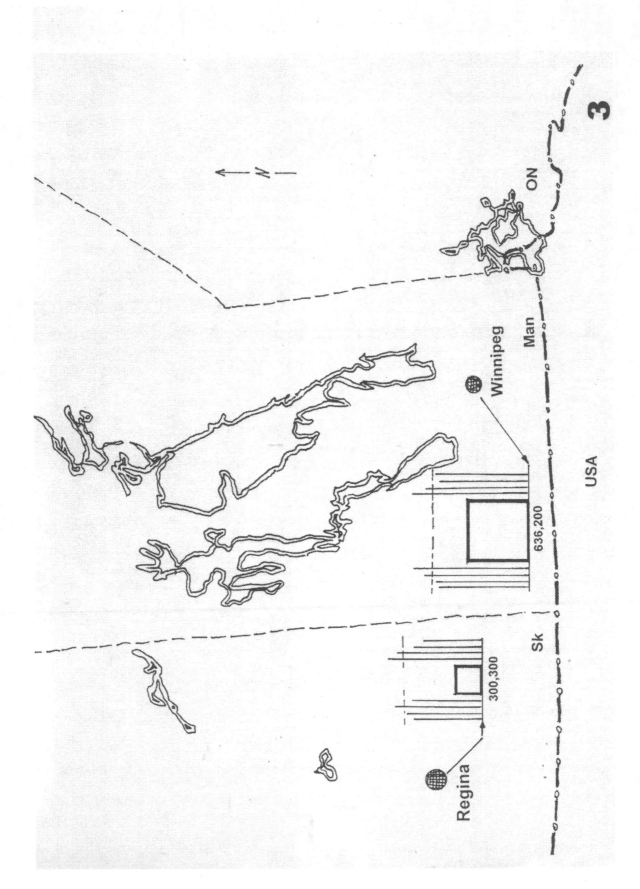

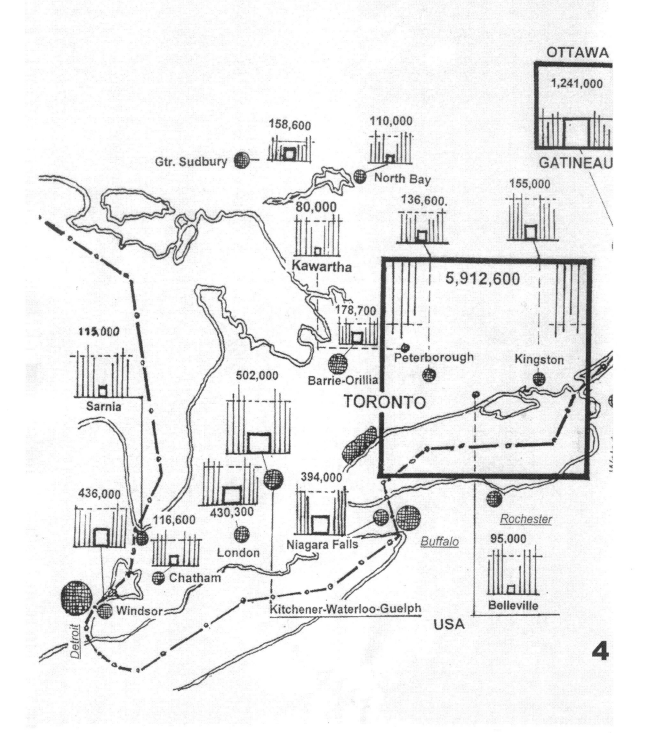

OTTAWA
1,241,000

GATINEAU

158,600
Gtr. Sudbury

110,000
North Bay

155,000

80,000
Kawartha

136,600

5,912,600

178,700

Peterborough   Kingston

115,000
Sarnia

Barrie-Orillia

TORONTO

502,000

436,000

116,600

430,300

London

394,000

Chatham

Niagara Falls

Rochester

Buffalo

95,000

Windsor

Kitchener-Waterloo-Guelph

Belleville

Detroit

USA

4

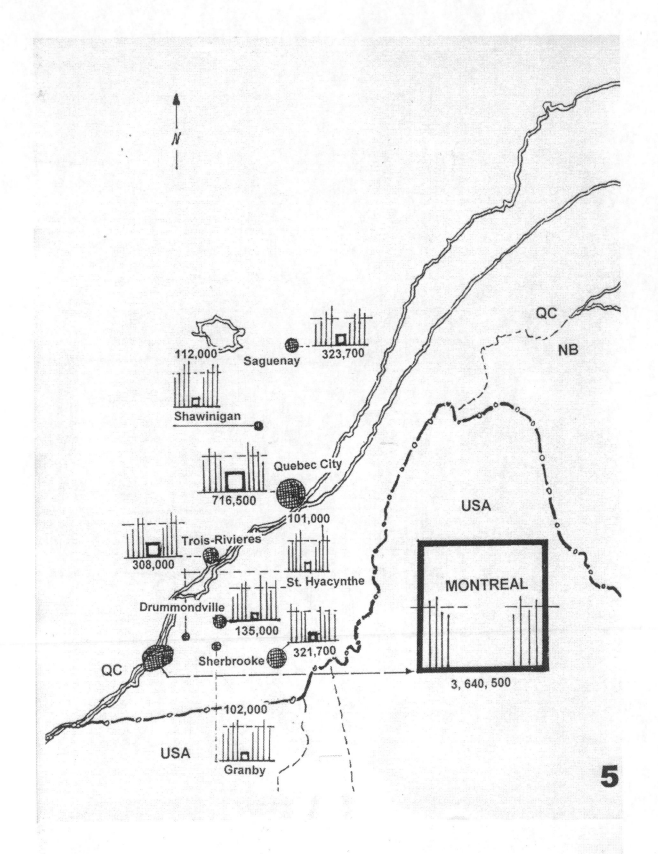

112,000
Saguenay
323,700

Shawinigan

Quebec City
716,500
101,000

Trois-Rivieres
308,000

St. Hyacynthe

Drummondville
135,000

321,700

MONTREAL
3, 640, 500

Sherbrooke

QC
102,000

USA
Granby

QC

NB

USA

5

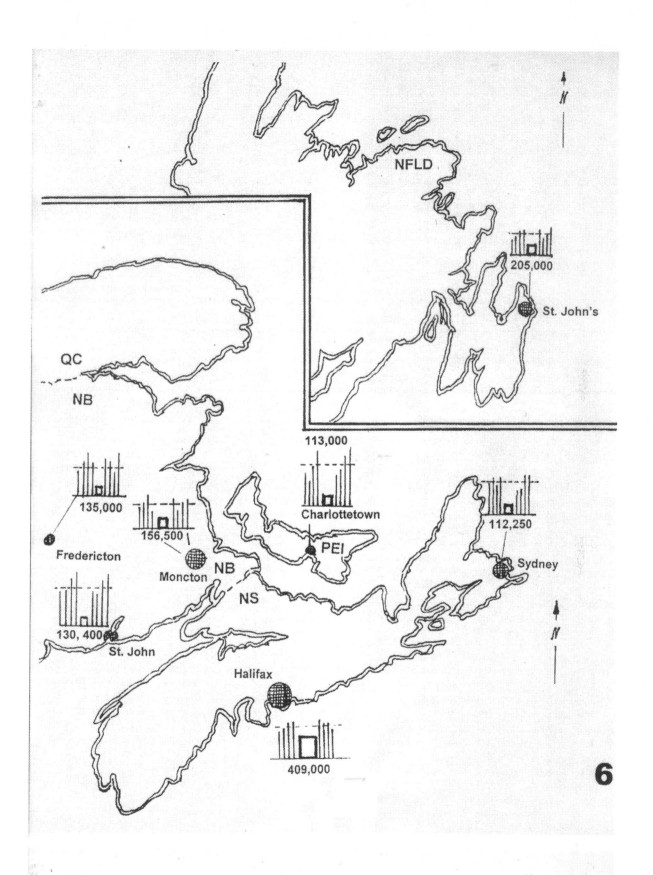

NFLD

205,000
St. John's

QC

NB

113,000

135,000

Fredericton

156,500

Charlottetown

112,250

Moncton

NB

PEI

Sydney

130,400

NS

St. John

Halifax

409,000

6

The 49 city regions shown on Table 1 are shown on maps here and in **alphabetical order**, complete with their Hinterland of small towns and villages within a 40-45 minutes' motoring distance from the city centre (2 inches on a straight line on the maps). After the city region's name, the total **"city region" population of "city+ settlements within a 40-45 minute motoring isochrone"** is given ; Four demographic tables giving their attributes of age, socio-economic, income and language (ie. cultural) variables; Description of the main activities, Functions, climate and other notable features. This whole area is referred to as a "market".

The text below the map of each market's name shows the collection of towns and villages forming the hinterland. The 4-column table below shows all the age, socio-economic, income, and language traits that should be considered when calculating the potential consumers for a particular product or service in that market. The estimation of a student population for primary and secondary education could be based on the age group data; the estimation of potential clients for a new car model, could be based on the professional and managerial socio-economic groups, while the marketing of a fashionable dress should be based not only on fashion shows at the city, but also on the relevant income and age groups. Finally, the marketing of a French book could be based on the proportion of speakers of that language group. Alternatively, four estimates could be produced by using the percentages on all population traits - age, s/e, income and language. Each of these four estimates may present a different total of Potential Consumers because each reflects a different angle of approach to the problem. The total derived from the relevant demographic characteristic, should be taken as the best expectation.

The last paragraph below the map shows the geographical and economic data relevant to service functions existing and worth considering before introducing an innovation at an affordable location in that city region. All the data given on the page - cartographic, demographic, numerical and textual - should help municipal officials, developers, entrepreneurs and interested consumers - to select the best locations for their project, product, service, or other - from building a new play area, to trading in diamonds, and from buying a particular product, to enjoying a holiday at a seaside hotel or ski motel.

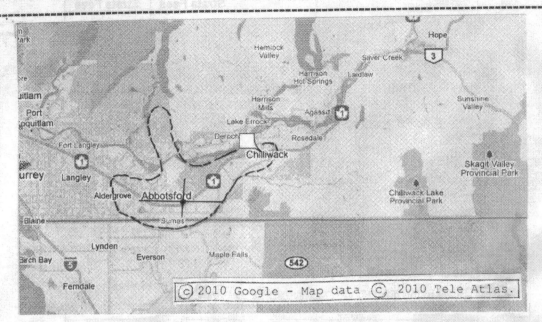

Abbotsford, Huntingdon, Aldergrove, Mission.

Age Structure		Socio-economics		$ Incomes		Languages	
0-19	92%	Mang/Prof	90%	10k-29k	116%	English	96%
20-24	96%	Clerical w.	110%	30k-49k	123%	French	1%
25-64	112%	Skilled w.	86%	50k-79k	8%	Chinese	1%
65+	108%	Others	107%	80k +	3%	Other	2%

The city has taken its name from a Scottish historic house by Sir Walter Scott, but the meaning of that name is related to the location of a "bridge for abbots" in BC. Much later, Erwin Singh Braich built a religious institution the Heritage Sikh Temple. It is the only early Sikh temple that has survived intact and today, "It is a site for all Canadians to visit and learn about Sikh history". The same benefactor has also built a sportsplex in his name.

The School of Integrated Arts is the only higher education establishment on published information.

Cultural facilities include the Abbotsford Theatre, Kariton Art Gallery, Reach Art Gallery & Museum and MSA Museum. Related to them are the Geological Society, a Theatre & Performing Arts Society and the Valley Covent Society.

Aware of the city's dependence on Vancouver, Abbotsford City Council has a very positive attitude to developers of entertainment facilities besides housing for an increasing number of commuters to that megalopolis.

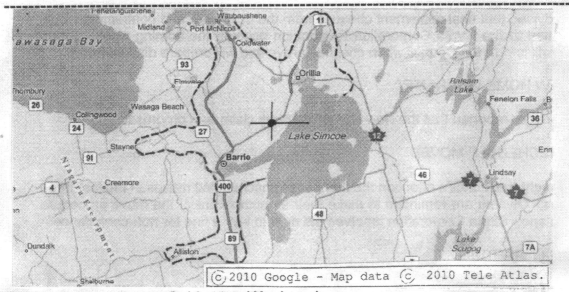

Barrie, Orillia, Alliston, Coldwater, Waubaushene

Age Structure		Socio-economics		$ Incomes		Languages	
0-19	128%	Mang/Prof	77%	10k-29k	108%	English	69%
20-24	85%	Clerical w	109%	30k-49k	131%	French	21%
25-64	106%	Skilled w	107%	50k-79k	82%	Chinese	7%
65+	79%	Others	111%	80k +	15%	Other	3%

Recent population growth by over 18% was due to inexpensive homes being built with many prefabricated structural components, low interest mortgages and jobs in great variety becoming available - from construction to ...baby care. Also e-mailing greatly facilitates owner-buyer meetings and deals being reached. Geographically, the favourable location of the new city between two lakes was bound to be exploited by entrepreneurs and municipalities.

The mild winter climate and fairly high temperatures of the area with clouds from the lakes bringing the occasional rain was also a factor in the city regions growth

The city of Barrie growing faster than Orillia, extended her bus service to cover the new development.

Orillia Opera House and a variety of social clubs satisfy the Cultural needs.

As regards entertainment, Casino Rama and pubs, but few other outlets. Nursery and junior classes, as in all new towns are overloaded. Playing fields are up to the municipalities to be enforced in sufficient number and area.

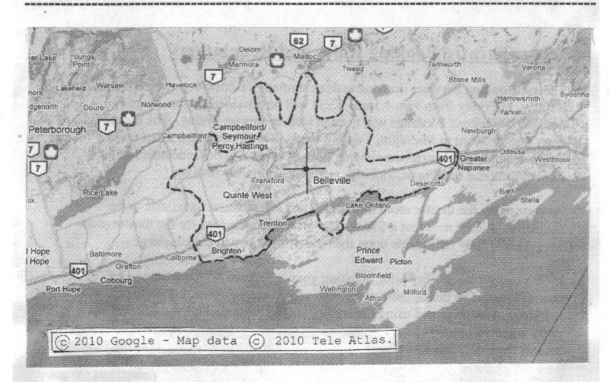

Brighton, Percy, Hastings, Greater Napanee, Desoronto, Trenton, Frankford, Quinte West

Age Structure		Socio-economics		$ Incomes		Languages	
0-19	98%	Mang/Prof	113%	10k-29k	38%	English	83%
20-24	107%	Clerical w	109%	30k-49k	94%	French	7%
25-64	112%	Skilled w	123%	50k-79k	16%	Chinese	6%
65+	121%	Others	121%	80k +	2%	Other	4%

The Toronto to Montreal route 401 bisects the city and Via Rail also traverses and stops there. This makes Belleville suitable for warehousing and any trade requiring fast freight transport to and from these two huge markets.   As a former lumber area, the city region has a large pool of skilled and semi-skilled labour.

For higher education, culture, hospital and specialized shopping, the city region is dependent on Toronto. Only local clinic and doctor surgeries are available.

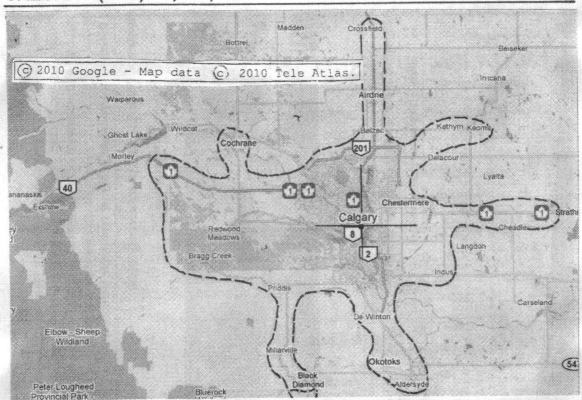

Calgary, Crossfield, Airdrie (fast growth), Balzac, Kathryn, Keonia, Delacour, Indus, Chestermere, Aldersyde, Okotoks (fast growth) , De Winton, Black Diamond, Leduc, Millarville, Priddis, Bragg Creek, Redwood Meadows, Cheadle, Cochrane, Strathcona.

Age Structure		Socio-economics		$ Incomes		Languages	
0-19	108%	Mang/Prof	132%	10k-29k	87%	English	79%
20-24	128%	Clerical w	117%	30k-49k	132%	French	9%
25-64	83%	Skilled w	121%	50k-79k	122%	Chinese	8%
65+	72%	Others	112%	80k +	52%	Other	4%

A major oil discovery and trading city region, outskirts of which are among the fastest growing in Canada.   Skilled immigrants are welcomed and services to them include home search, school search, language teaching, health, justice and social services. Particularly welcome are computer trained young and able to carry out computer servicing for business and institutions within 115 miles from Calgary Tower at city centre. Prov. taxes are minimal. the outlook positive.

The University of Calgary has 75 partner institutions in 25 countries. Bow Valley College and several others.

Cultural facilities include the Aero Space Museum, Calgary Highlander Museum, Calgary Science Centre, Heritage Park Historic Village and Leduc "Oil Sands Discovery Centre", Festivals: Calgary Stampede, Chuck Wagon Races.
Entertainment in casinos, night clubs, luxury hotel lounge bars and many pubs.

The city region enjoys 2,300 hrs of sunshine per annum, but plenty of snow too.

CHARLOTTETOWN (PEI)   113.000

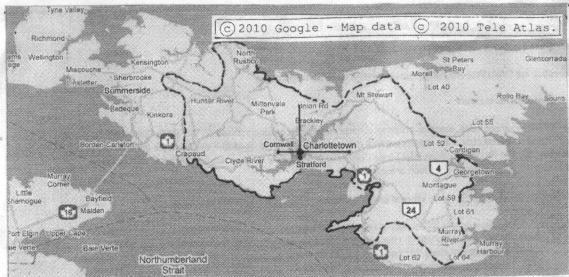

Charlottetown, Stratford, Crapaud, North Rustica, Miltonvale Park, Union Rd, Brackley, Mt Stewart, Lot 52, Cardigan, Georgetown, Montague, Lot 59, Lot 64.

Age Structure		Socio-economics		$ Incomes		Languages	
0-19	87%	Mang/Prof	82%	10k-29k	142%	English	51%
20-24	93%	Clerical w	90%	30k-49k	95%	French	42%
25-64	96%	Skilled w	121%	50k-79k	61%	Chinese	6%
65+	145%	Others	143%	80k +	5%	Other	1%

An agricultural city region, with an extensive hinterland and a particular sense of place. It may be the smallest Provincial capital, but it has room and scope to expand, by virtue of its fertile soil and nation-wide market of potatoes. The bridge connection to the mainland was a much debated link, but it is proving its worth every day - for exports to, as well as imports from the Island.

No university has yet been established as neighbouring Moncton and Halifax appear to satisfy the island's needs.

Cultural facilities are the Confederation Centre of the Arts, containing a theatre, art gallery and a museum. Historic Government House (1834) and Beaconsfield (1877) overlook the city's harbour. Little commercial freight, but a great many recreational craft use that harbour. It will have to grow considerably to urge the provision of Port Functions outined earlier in this book.

As regards recreation, Prince Edward Island National Park with visitor centres at Cavendish and Dalway, has some of North America's finest beaches. Red sandstone cliffs more than 30 meteres high, stretch from North Rustico Harbour to Orby Head. At Brackley Beach, walkways wind through 18-metre high sand dunes. Dalvay-by-the-Sea was the 1895 elegant summer home of American oil tycoon named Dalvay.

Japanese tourists visit the house of Anne of Green Gables by the busload every summer, for their love of the novel and Anne....

Wallaceburg, Thames, Blenheim, Tilbury, Bell River

Age Structure		Socio-economics		$ Incomes		Languages	
0-19	98%	Mang/Prof	123%	10k-29k	38%	English	83%
20-24	117%	Clerical w	109%	30k-49k	104%	French	7%
25-64	111%	Skilled w	113%	50k-79k	26%	Chinese	6%
65+	121%	Others	101%	80k +	5%	Other	4%

Diverse in economy, this city region has a base in agriculture and car part production, thanks to its proximity to US Great Lake industrial complex. It is also an intermediate transport station between Windsor and Toronto and aims to become a "Green technology hub".

The climate is mild and sunny, but the manufacture of car parts produces slight pollution

Beyond the existing public library, the recently established Cultural Centre - for some - or Entertainment Complex - for others - is a varied and continuously developing facility, offering an art gallery, live theatre, heritage museum, life science and education classes, swimming pool, pub, cafes, sports, and multi-cultural cuisine restaurant. The Complex is designed to attract US families for day trips, like the West Edmonton Mall.

The Motor City Speedway caters for car racing enthusiasts.

Retirement and long-care homes cater for the high proportion of elderly persons.

A most promising city region catering for her own people and beyond.

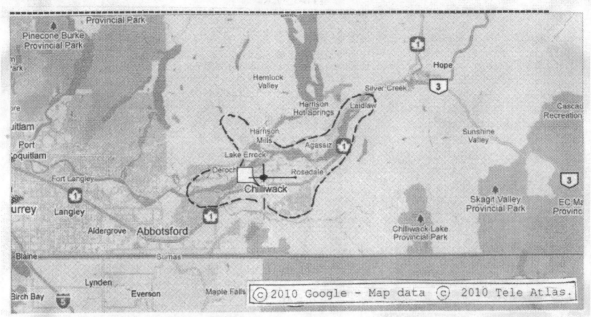

Chilliwack, Mission, Deroche, Agassiz, Hope.

Age Structure		Socio-economics		$ Incomes		Languages	
0-19	81%	Mang/Prof	109%	10k-29k	71%	English	89%
20-24	104%	Clerical w	82%	30k-49k	92%	French	3%
25-64	68%	Skilled w	117%	50k-79k	9%	Chinese	2%
65+	137%	Others	127%	80k +	1%	Other	6%

Guarding the valuable green space separating this city from the growing mega-lopolis of Vancouver, the Chamber of Commerce directs development away from that green zone. The proportion of elderly residents is continuously growing however and only commuters add to her population.   If chosen as an out-of-town location for a major facility, it may well be successful if it satisfies the large number of retirees.

A museum of local history, Chilliwack Museum illustrates the phase-by-phase growth of the town, while the Minter Gardens show different floral arrangements on various themes. There is also an aviary and a petting zoo. At CFB Chilliwack there is a Canadian Military Museum with Boer War, WWII and other Canadian participation displays. Nearby Hope town has a visitors' centre with a Friendship Gardenand the abandoned Othello-Quitette Tunnels - ancient railway tunnel. Huge roadside boulders have formed the 1965 Hope Slide, when an avalanche buried the road in 45 metres of rubble.

All entertainment and specialized shopping desires are directed to Vancouver.

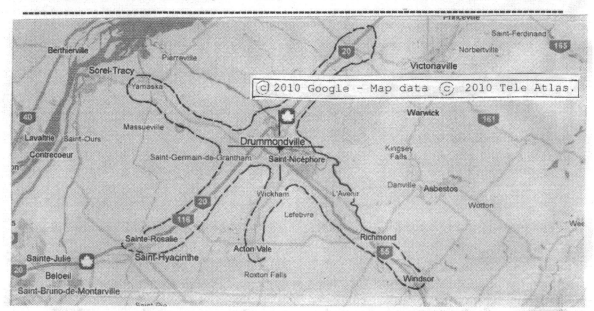

Yamaska, St, Gillaume d'Upton, St. Jude, St. Hyacinthe, Acton Vale, Richmond,
Saint-Nicephore

Age Structure		Socio-economics		$ Incomes		Languages	
0-19	81%	Mang/Prof	127%	10k-29k	57%	English	9%
20-24	87%	Clerical w	109%	30k-49k	92%	French	79%
25-64	118%	Skilled w	97%	50k-79k	19%	Chinese	4%
65+	122%	Others	110%	80k +	2%	Other	8%

A small population centre when the Empire Loyalists arrived from USA in the 1760-ies, this town
grew considerably when neighbouring Asbestos village found its cancer-generating product usable
for building fireproofing purposes. But the sale and mining were soon legislated against and both
village and town had to diversify their industries to economically survive. Nowadays Drummondville grows at the rate of 3.8% /annum and her residential density = 652.3 p/km sq.

A Drummondville Community Improvement Plan has been adopted and signs of improvement and
started to appear after the involvement of Katimavik youth.   City hall keeps a good consultant to
provide advice to entrepreneurs and economic studies of the agri-food   sector have been started.
Exhibition of new and inexpensive homes is often being organized to gain new residents and older
persons find it ideal for retirement. Paper pulp as a by product of the forest industry has recently
flourished. The city region needs more facilities on culture and entertainment

The climate is "relatively temperate" in winter as well as summer.

EDMONTON (Alta)   935,000

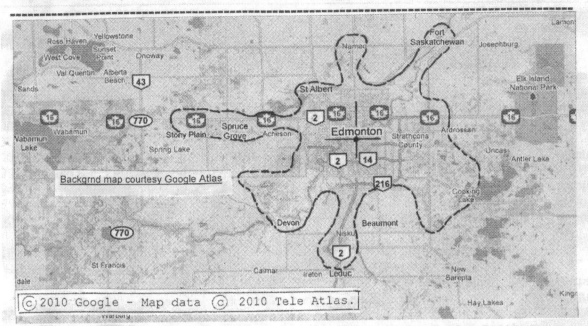

Edmonton, Devon, Acheson, Spruce Grove, Stony Plain, St. Albert, Namao, Fort Saskatchewan, Strathcona County, Cooking Lake, Nisku, Leduc.

Age Structure		Socio-economics		$ Incomes		Languages	
0-19	99%	Mang/Prof	129%	10k-29k	29%	English	78%
20-24	94%	Clerical w	118%	30k-49k	102%	French	6%
25-64	121%	Skilled w	97%	50k-79k	14%	Chinese	3%
65+	87%	Others	113%	80k +	9%	Other	13%

The city is "an economic powerhouse and hotbed for entrepreneurs" trying to capture wider markets through less costly services and products (low gasoline prices).

Since formation in Jan1993 the Edmonton Economic Development Council has introduced coherent objectives by emphasizing entertainment next to existing functions of Prov'l Administration, Education (University and colleges) Health, Culture (Citadel Theatre, Alta Prov Museum, Leduc Oil Sand Interpretative Center, Art Gallery) and Specialized shopping (West Edmonton Mall - attracting US visitors since 1981) to help growth in Tourism services. The Mall is a very imaginative private development including secondary education, entertainment and other varied facilities, to keep shoppers - particularly youngsters - for the whole day). The climate is moderate continental with fairly hot summer days.

EEDC has introduced innovative programs (Golf for Women), detailed city guides, mini golf, skating rinks and a roller coaster - landmarks. to earn the city the name "Canada's Festival City".

FREDERICTON (NB)   135,000

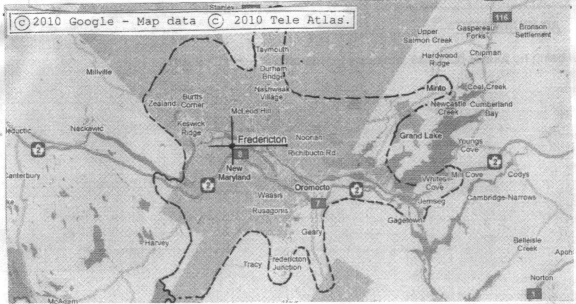

Fredericton, Fiume Ridge, Zealand, Keswick Ridge, Burits Corner, Noonan, Oromocto, Waasis, Jemseg, Rusagonis, Geary, Fredericton Junction, Taymouth, White's Cove, Gagetown, Minto, Richinycto Road, Nashwaak Village, Durham Ridge, Nashwaak Bridge.

Age Structure		Socio-economics		$ Incomes		Languages	
0-19	91%	Mang/Prof	133%	10k-29k	127%	English	59%
20-24	123%	Clerical w	125%	30k-49k	118%	French	29%
25-64	143%	Skilled w	86%	50k-79k	67%	Chinese	3%
65+	110%	Others	144%	80k +	1%	Other	9%

A vibrant city with airport and frequent air services, providing access to USA and Canadian markets, It is centre to many Federal and Provincial offices and its "Daily Gleaner" is read widely in NB. The University (shared with St. John) concentrates on social research and training schools serve a wide area. The Community College has a network of branches providing customized training for community work. Links with Bowater Co., Canadian Forest Service and Nova Scotia's Department of Natural Resources enable University research on how to integrate socio-economic issues with forestry production and foreseeable climate changes and geographic phenomena (global warming, tides, etc.)

Humid continental climate with January being the coldest and July the warmest month in New Brunswick.

The learning institutions help to keep the 20-24 age group at par with the Canadian average but the 65+ group are predominant.

Forestry for exports and gardening to save money on food costs. The surviving Acadian legacy of New Brunswick makes it the only officially bilingual province.

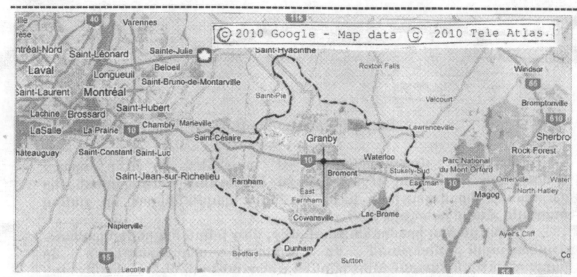

Ganby city, Waterloo, Stukey-sud, Eastman, East Farnham, Bromont, Saint-Cesaire

Age Structure		Socio-economics		$ Incomes		Languages	
0-19	87%	Mang/Prof	117%	10k-29k	37%	English	6%
20-24	97%	Clerical w	99%	30k-49k	62%	French	79%
25-64	118%	Skilled w	127%	50k-79k	9%	Chinese	4%
65+	124%	Others	114%	80k +	2%	Other	11%

First settled by three brothers named Frost, but City preferred to take the name of a 1920-30 prize fighter. City status won in 1971 and invited new industries to add to existing textile, lumber and dairy product industries. A Province-wide structural steel truss and other products is also active in Granby.   A Magistrate's Court sits at Granby.

A famous driving instruction firm has established a school to train police and other emergency driver how to drive safely. A busy library is run by the municipality. Visited fairly often are the Museum of Canadian History and the heritage attraction homes of famous citizens of older days.   Quality restaurants, hotels, pubs and restaurants meet the demand by resident s and tourists.

The most widely known and profitable facility is the Granby Zoo, due to numerous species maintained and because the bikeways through the Zoo are very popular with families. Particularly popular is the annual festival of mascot animals - Fete des Mascottes. Other recreational facilities are the Municipal Arena for ice hockey and private golf course.

The growth of local tourism due to increasing airfares, adds considerably to attractions like Granby Zoo, but greater publicity could make the cultural facilities more attractive to tourists.   Climate is cod with a fair amount of snow in winter, but moderate in summer.

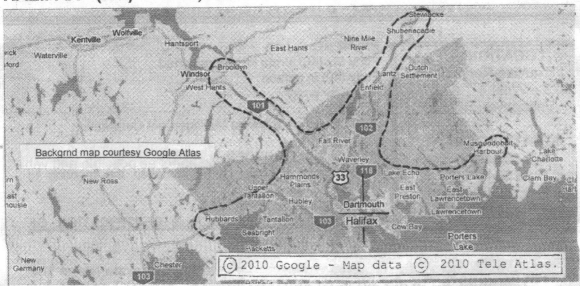

Backgrnd map courtesy Google Atlas

© 2010 Google - Map data © 2010 Tele Atlas.

Dartmouth, Halifax, Hubley, Hammonds Plains, Upper Tantalion, Tantalion, Hubbards, Seabright, Hackets Cove, Indian Harbour, Brooklyn, Windsor, Waverly, Enfield, Hubley, Lantz, Shubenacadie, Stewacke, West Hants, Cow Bay, Fall River, Lake Echo, East Preston, Porters Lake, Lawrencetown + East Lawrencetown, Musquodobolt Harbour.

Age Structure		Socio-economics		$ Incomes		Languages	
0-19	91%	Mang/Prof	121%	10k-29k	115%	English	79%
20-24	98%	Clerical w	113%	30k-49k	108%	French	11%
25-64	119%	Skilled w	112%	50k-79k	77%	Chinese	8%
65+	123%	Others	89%	80k +	6%	Other	2%

Halifax, major centre of Atlantic Canada's economy has been called the "fifth best location in the world for good business".   She is attracting many companies and much office development. Some of the 5 Canadian banks - all major national developers - were founded in this city. Halifax averages 196 foggy days per year and the climate of Nova Scotia, has spring temperatures from 1 to 17 degrees, in summer varying from 14 to 25 degrees, in autumn they vary from 5 to 20 degrees and in winter from -11 to 5 degrees.

Nova Scotia's history started about 5,000 BC with the arrival of the Micmac.   It became the "new land of the Scots" only after the expulsion of over 12,000 Acadians by the British in 1755. Some 30,000 Empire Loyalists were shared by New Brunswick -14,000 - and Nova Scotia and both won many new enterprises. Halifax and Dartmouth are home to universities - Dalhousie, King's College, Mount St Vincent, St Mary's - and colleges from the Atlantic Sc. of Theology to the College of Art & Design. The total student population in 2006 amounted to 29, 535.

Fisheries were the economy's pillar, but after the loss of 20,000 jobs in 1992 due to depletion, small business made up 92,5% of all employment, with Tourism being second, Info Tech third (15.000 jobs), Film production fourth and Insurance fifth.   Low pop growth projection (7.7% btwn 1991 and 2021 while Canada expected to add 37.6%). Proportion of age 65+ group is quite high while that of the 0-19 group is low.

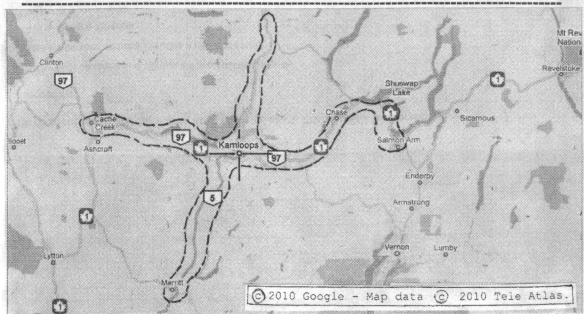

Kamloops, Barriere, Chase, Monte Creek, North Kamloops, South Thompson, Kamloops Lake

Age Structure		Socio-economics		$ Incomes		Languages	
0-19	98%	Mang/Prof	93%	10k-29k	38%	English	83%
20-24	108%	Clerical w	104%	30k-49k	94%	French	7%
25-64	112%	Skilled w	113%	50k-79k	16%	Chinese	6%
65+	131%	Others	124%	80k +	2%	Other	4%

A transportation hub by virtue of rail, road and air routes cris-crossing at Kamloops . An important rail station on the TransCanada Via Rail toute; a Regional Airport for flights, in and out of the BC borders makes this city region accessible world wide. Finally the cross-shaped city region is due to important cross-road in the city. The economy is diversified economy with manufactures, agriculture (wheat, alfa-alfa) fruit cultivation, forestry - timber supply area with Douglas fir cultivation expanding northwards but many services is also rapidly growing. Some of the above industries advertise the jobs which may only be filled by outsiders and among the relocation services, there are also some incentives like homes, apartments and land.

Livestock producers are headquartered in Kamloops - seat of BC livestock Producers Co-op Association. Vegetation, animal and forest cultivation are modernized.
As regards Tourism, there are no built facilities but in terms of nature walks, many trails culminate at the refreshing sight of waterfalls. The mild, dry climate and relaxed lifestyle in many parts of the city region are rather deceptive, because some reports emphasize the need for government funded services to support the population.

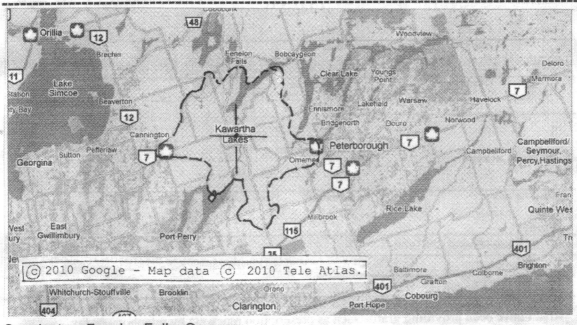

Cannington, Fanelon Falls, Omeme

Age Structure		Socio-economics		$ Incomes		Languages	
0-19	115%	Mang/Prof	77%	10k-29k	4%	English	79%
20-24	87%	Clerical w	89%	30k-49k	92%	French	9%
25-64	108%	Skilled w	157%	50k-79k	9%	Chinese	2%
65+	82%	Others	110%	80k +	2%	Other	1 0%

Midway between two lakes, this city has a small catchment now, but the building of new roads and villages will gradually enlarge and enhance the market around it. As a recently established City, her municipality has started opening new Divisions and among the earliest was the Parks, Recreation and Culture Division. It has also unveiled a memorial for the Trent-Severn Waterway - Canada's highest body of fresh water.

Location at the crossing of highways 7 and 35 gives access to Lake Simcoe and Metro Toronto, the latter increasing the city region's dependence on the great variety of goods and services of that megalopolis. Nevertheless, the new city presents opportunities for entrepreneurs to develop not only new housing but also novel facilities - for culture and entertainment, shopping and recreation, health and higher education from infrastructure to superstructure of all Functions. Current low farmland prices should favour this.

The municipality favours the establishment of diverse industries, be they manufactures or services. The region enjoys mild winters and warm summers and some imaginative lakeside facilities should increase the tourist appeal of the whole area. An historic inn and country club located at the heart of the region has a great appeal already.

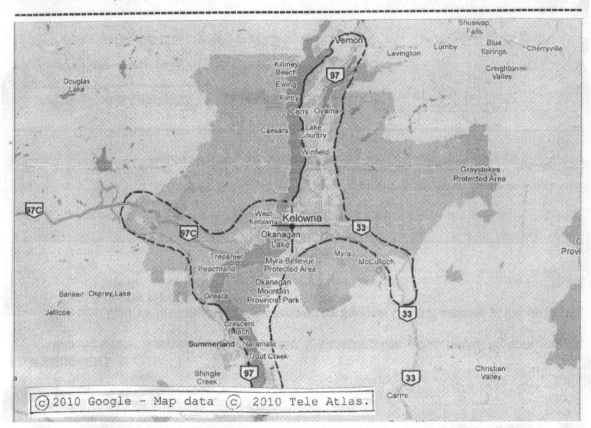

Kelowna, Vernon, Oyama, Carrs, Lake Country, Winfield, Okanagan, Greata, Myra, Penticton, Trout Creek, Naramata, Crscent Beach, Peachland, Trepanier, McCulloch.

Age Structure		Socio-economics		$ Income		Languages	
0-19	91%	Mang/Prof	113%	10k-29k	77%	English	68%
20-24	123%	Clerical w	122%	30k-49k	108%	French	19%
25-64	133%	Skilled w	86%	50k-79k	37%	Chinese	4%
65+	140%	Others	144%	80k +	1%	Other	9%

Well-established inland retirement resort in British Columbia and Alberta, the city region is famous for wine production, some 30 producers being BC Wine Institute members . Fruit are plentiful and both wine and fruit are exported well beyond BC. Retail, tourism and retirement services form the fastest growing sector of the economy. Aerospace, high tech and investment services are also growing - economically most promising. Mild climate and almost daily bright sunshine allows swimming, boating and sailing in the lengthy and busy Okanagan lake. Llively agriculture, forestry, tourism and retail services prevail also in Vernon, Pentincton and West Kelowna, the latter providing all camping requirements. Cultural facilities are the Art Gallery, Okanagan Butterfly World and BC Orchard Industry Museum, Centennial Museum and sculptures. Entertainment in quality restaurants, luxury hotel lounges and cinemas leaves all visitors happy.

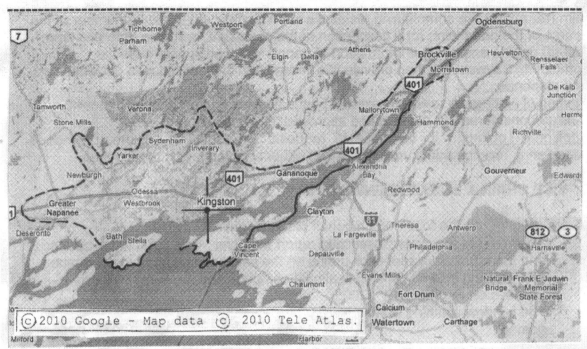

Kingston, Cape Vincent, Gananoque, Mailorytown, Mallorytown, Morristown, Inverary, Sydenham, Yarker, Newburgh, Greater Napanee, Bath, Brockville, Stella.

Age Structure		Socio-economics		$ Incomes		Languages	
0-19	121%	Mang/Prof	109%	10k-29k	69%	English	83%
20-24	107%	Clerical w	79%	30k-49k	29%	French	12%
25-64	69%	Skilled w	107%	50k-79k	11%	Chinese	2%
65+	121%	Others	124%	80k +	7%	Other	3%

Former capital of Canada with many historic buildings and statues. Today, it is a sailing port for boats arriving from the north and for yachts arriving from either side of the St. Lawrence Seaway.

Gateway to the Thousand Islands and the St. Lawrence Islands National Park.

Attractions include the 19th century City Hall, the International Ice Hockey Museum, Marine Museum of the Great Lakes, Fort Henry, Bellevue House National Historic Site preserving the residence of Canada's first Prime Minister, Sir John A. Macdonald.

Kingston city region's climate is humid in winter with occasional snow, but warm days in summer.

Market town with great potential in tourism.

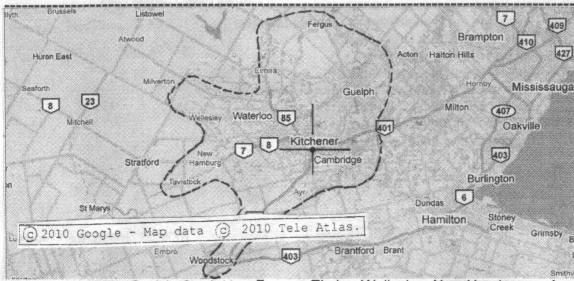

Kitchener, Waterloo, Guelph, Cambridge, Fergus, Elmira, Wellesley, New Hambourg, Ayr, Tavistock, Woodstock.

Age Structure		Socio-economics		$ Incomes		Languages	
0-19	97%	Mang/Prof	132%	10k-29k	54%	English	80%
20-24	118%	Clerical w	127%	30k-49k	107%	French	9%
25-64	141%	Skilled w	129%	50k-79k	31%	Chinese	5%
65+	112%	Others	77%	80k +	7%	Other	6%

With ½ a million people in 4 coalescing cities, KWCG city region is a developing Canadian megalopolis ("Canada's Technology Triangle") and high family incomes well above the Ontario median. The Triangle is in effect, a technopolis with a Research Park and with Cambridge space travel hardware manufacture as part of the complex. The brainpower is evident in the above s/e column above.

Higher education is provided by 3 universities and numerous technical colleges. Jobs are advertised in 4 dailies and vacancies are soon filled with young technologists. Among other signs of future growth are the reliance on computer manufacturing - rather than old industries - the encouragement of youth culture (music groups and clubs) and the welcoming municipalities (employing 30,000) always waiting for new entrepreneurs, to offer them inexpensive land, earmarked for infotech development. Banks readily provide inexpensive mortgages to first-time home buyers.   Municipal transit bus services and railways help to reduce commuter and in-city car traffic. Among progressive municipal moves, the Multicultural Centre land in which ethnic groups may develop their cultural centre and celebrate their historical feasts and cuisine is perhaps the most practical example of Trudeau's policy.

Cultural and more lately, Entertainment facilities are attracting grants and investment. Guelph has 4,000; Cambridge 1,920; and Kitchener 4,715 cultural heritage buildings, operated as cultural venues and vital Tourist attractions. Municipalities may soon be amalgamated to attract more Provincial and private funds according to an Econ. Develop't Strategy.   An active Youth Music Centre in Guelph, Laurier Faculty of Music, Kitchener Art Gallery, the 25,000 sq ft "Funworx", Waterloo City Museum, Kitchener Waterloo Symphony Orchestra and the $187,000 grant to develop more cultural and art facilities are all signs of the emphasis placed on cultural development.

Recreational facilities in community centres, the Grand River Conservation project, the Golf Tournament, Waterloo Field Naturalists - all indicate respect for open green space and refusal to see it disappear under the pressure of rapid growth.

The high proportion of 65+ elderly is shown by the Meals-On-Wheels services in many districts.

LETHBRIDGE (Alta)   175,000

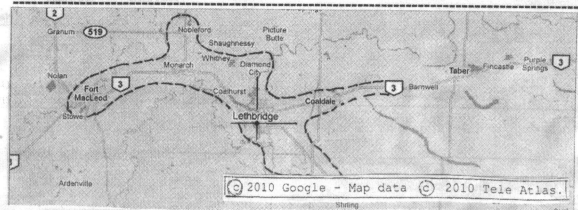

© 2010 Google - Map data © 2010 Tele Atlas.

Lethbridge, Stirling, Coaldale, Diamond City, Whitney, Monarch, Barbwell, Coalhurst, Fort MacLeod, Nobleford.

Age Structure		Socio-economics		$ Incomes		Languages	
0-19	108%	Mang/Prof	96%	10k-29k	36%	English	84%
20-24	109%	Clerical w	107%	30k-49k	97%	French	12%
25-64	110%	Skilled w	112%	50k-79k	17%	Chinese	1%
65+	89%	Others	126%	80k +	2%	Other	3%

Formerly an agriculture-based industry town, The city's economy developed from drift mines opened in 1874, making it the main marketing, distribution and centre in southern Alberta. Today she has three main pillars of economy - agriculture, coal mining and the University   A February 2010 conference concluded that diversification of the City's economy   should be treated as a priority, the Federal economic program should encourage the establishment of new industries.

The University was a prime mover in attracting new informatics industries and students from all over the Province and beyond are attracted. Soon after the City established a Chamber of Commerce, new housing was built..

Culturally, the Galt Museum & Archives and at the western end of the city region, Fort Macleod and Fort Whoop-up museums attract some tourists, but not as many as the "Head-Smashed -in Buffalo Jump" which is a UNESCO World Heritage Site, as a monument to the ingenuity of man in hunting and freezing meat, to survive the following winter.

Nikka Yuko Japanese Gardens, local parks and playgrounds cater for recreational needs, but there is little other than pubs and restaurants for entertainment.

The climate is   mild in winter and summer days are cool thanks to the chinook

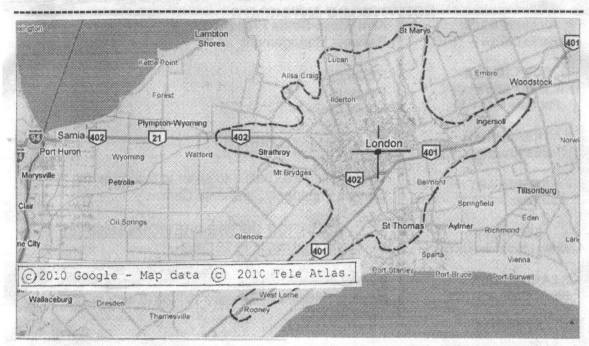

London, Ingersoll, St.Thomas, Belmont, Dutton, Wallacetown, Rodney, West Lorne, Mt. Brydges, Strathroy, Ilderton, Lucan, St.Mary's

Age Structure		Socio-economics		$ Incomes		Languages	
0-19	109%	Mang/Prof	136%	10k-29k	51%	English	78%
20-24	122%	Clerical w	104%	30k-49k	108%	French	11%
25-64	106%	Skilled w	96%	50k-79k	29%	Chinese	6%
65+	104%	Others	102%	80k +	9%	Other	4%

One of Canada's fast growing cities (3.6% / annum) and the third fastest in Ontario. Main industries include General Motors Defense contracts, Siemens Electric, 3M and Kelogg.

The University of West Ontario has been consistently rated as among the best and has links with Canada's Technology Triangle nearby (see KWCG). Art College, Design schools, Dance schools and many other learning places for a youthful population well above the National average (122%). Among cultural facilities, notable is the theatre and performance arts club.

The city region has many heritage sites as it has featured in many events related to Canadas' history. Museums, Art Galleries, Commercial galleries, Special libraries - all very accessible.

Entertainment facilities include night clubs, cinemas, quality restaurants

Recreational facilities and parks contain playgrounds, children play areas. Sports and stadiums cater for university and college students as well as other young residents.

The climate is mild in winter as well as summer.

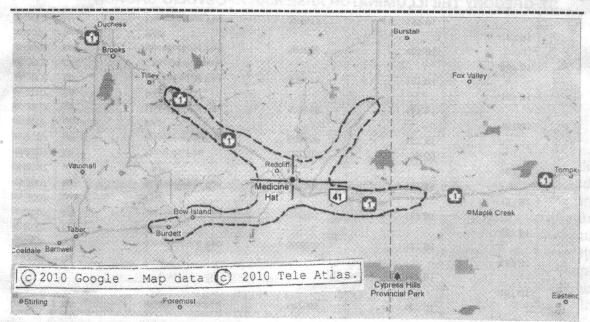

Medicine Hat, Ralston, Suffield, Redcliff, Irvinne, Walsh, Whitla, Saanichton, Sidney, Mill Bay, Fullford Harbour, Bow Island

Age Structure		Socio-economics		$ Incomes		Languages	
0-19	83%	Mang/Prof	75%	10k-29k	48%	English	75%
20-24	111%	Clerical w	105%	30k-49k	104%	French	9%
25-64	74%	Skilled w	117%	50k-79k	11%	Chinese	2%
65+	119%	Others	129%	80k +	2%	Other	14%

Home of the South Alberta Light Horse military base which contributes some C$120 million to the local economy.   Wheat and other agricultural production is the other important base of the city's economy with greenhouse production advancing rapidly.

Among the most important services run by the municipality is the Commerce Chamber and bus network helping to connect producers and clients in hinterland and central city.

Cultural facilities are the Medicine Hat Museum and Art Gallery. Major contributors to Alberta's ethnic diversity have been the European immigrants who worked hard after getting their land entitlement. In this city region, they form a high percentage of the population and produce the lion's share of wheat production for export.

The climate is semi-arid steppe with mild winters and hot summer days.

Saamis Teepee is the most visible landmark in the city region and it was originally built for the 1988 Calgary Winter Olympics. It measures 215 ft. in height and it has lateral supports to withstand strong winds frequent in the area.

MONCTON (NB)   156,500

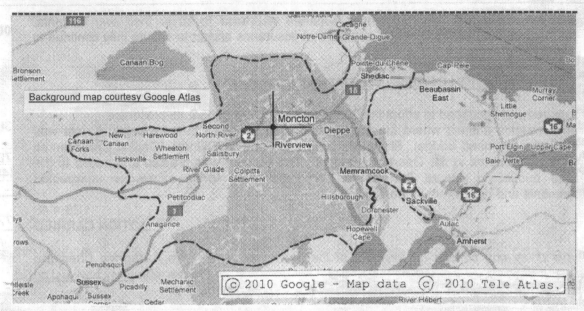

Background map courtesy Google Atlas

© 2010 Google - Map data © 2010 Tele Atlas.

Moncton, Cacagne, Notre Dame, Grande Digue, Pointe du Chene, Shediac, Memramcook, Sackville, Hillsborough, Dorchester, Hopewell Cape, Anagance, Petitcodiac, River Glade, Salisbury, Wheaton Settlement, Hicksville, New Canaan, Canaan Forks, Harewood, Dieppe, Second North River, Riverview.

Age Structure		Socio-economics		$ Incomes		Languages	
0-19	92%	Mang/Prof	124%	10k-29k	135%	English	56%
20-24	103%	Clerical w	76%	30k-49k	106%	French	27%
25-64	138%	Skilled w	99%	50k-79k	89%	Chinese	8%
65+	77%	Others	111%	80k +	3%	Other	9%

Metro Moncton has a varied service industry serving the city region and that was quite a difficult transition from ship-building. The busiest airport in New Brunswick has been based in Moncton and it is expected to act as the city region's economic prime mover.
Pilot training courses are quite popular for professional as well as recreational purposes.
In manufactures, Maple Leaf Foods in Moncton industrial park provides many jobs.
Moncton hospital offers major services in Trauma, Neurosurgery, Burns, Oncology and infectious diseases - skills which the local doctors have developed over many years, while the city region was primarily occupied in ship-building. Thus, Health and Welfare functions are traditional to the region.

Among the most popular cultural groups, the Atlantic Ballet Opera is based in Moncton.

On Recreation, the playing fields and sports facilities are well and frequently used, but a second major sporting venue appears to be essential in Moncton, particularly as the city will host the world during the IAAF World Junior Championships.
Climate is cold and continental in the inland areas, but mild and maritime during the summers, with January being coldest and July the warmest months.

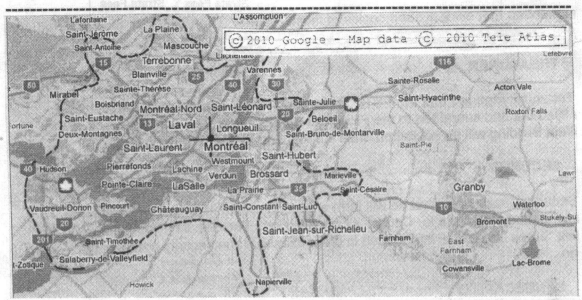

Montreal, Longueuil, Laval, Montreal-Nord, St. Leonard, Ste-Julie, Hudson, Blainville, La Plaine
Salaberry, Brossard, Verdun, Lachine, La Prairie, Marienville, Pincourt, Chateauguay, La Salle,
Pointe-Claire, Vaudreuil-Dorion, Pierrefonds, Deux Montagnes, Mirabel, Boisbriand, Westmount,
Mascouche, Lachine, Repentigny, Varennes, Napierville and Sts Antoine, Jerome, Leonard, Cesaire,
Constant, Bruno, Eustache, Hubert, Luc, Julie, Therese et Timothee.

Age Structure		Socio-economics		$ Incomes		Languages	
0-19	110%	Mang/Prof	106%	10k-29k	81%	English	11%
20-24	123%	Clerical w	121%	30k-49k	136%	French	69%
25-64	92%	Skilled w	123%	50k-79k	134%	Chinese	4%
65+	89%	Others	132%	80k +	31%	Other	16

Montreal's stock exchange (2nd to TSX) heads Finance. 260 companies make it 3rd in the world
(Seattle and Toulouse) in aerospace. Info-tech employs 100,000 in 2008; Computer tech
60,000; Multinational tech co's (110) had 13,000, while 130 biotech companies employ 4,700;
Some 380 companies on health employ 24,550 employees. Some 330,000 are employed by
34,000 companies in tourism, and Alcan is the world's 2nd largest aluminum producer.

Education is headed by two Universities - Quebec and Sherbrooke - l'Ecole Polytechnique,
Dawson and many other colleges are preparing students for more computer brainwork.

Cultural attractions include the Symphony Orchestra, Jardin Botanique, Centre Canadien
d'Architecture, d'Histoire, d'Art, Chapelle Notre-Dame-de-Bonsecours, Planetarium and others.
Numerous festivals are held starting with Fete de Neiges, at places like le Vieux Montreal, le
vieux Port, Lac de deux Montagnes, etc. Tourists come for conventions (3rd most popular in
North America) numerous historic sites and literary events. Entertainment has famous Irish and
German pubs, the annual Jazz Festival, film Festivals, many nightclubs, discotheques, dance
clubs, stylish lounges and luxury hotels.

Specialized shopping, particularly Designer Closeout Sales in Reso de la ville, a 30 km network

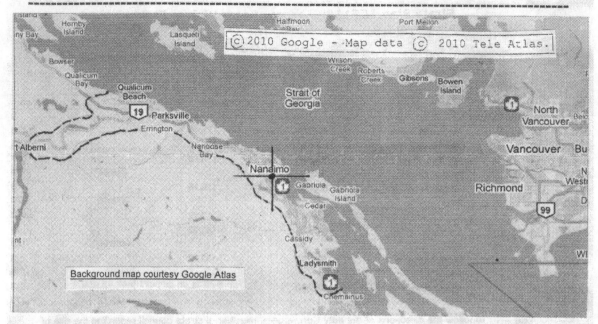

Background map courtesy Google Atlas

Nanaimo, Ladysmith, Nanoose Bay, Port Alberni.

Age Structure		Socio-economics		$ Incomes		Languages	
0-19	95%	Mang/Prof	88%	10k-29k	77%	English	51%
20-24	119%	Clerical w	96%	30k-49k	48%	French	10%
25-64	97%	Skilled w	113%	50k-79k	39%	Chinese	18%
65+	132%	Others	124%	80k +	3%	Other	21%

Founded as a trading post in 1849, after discovery and mining of coal, the "Nanaimo Bastion" started to export it. Next stage was to build a commercial fishing fleet, trade farm produce and saw lumber. An Oceanographic Research Station is now a main employer. Nanaimo is known as the "Hub city" (virtually at Vancouver Island's central city) colloquially, "Hub, Tub and Pub" city. It is frequently linked by ferry and hydro-plane to Vancouver and Victoria. Median household income = $46,000 (BC = $52,709.

Vancouver Island University is centred in Nanaimo and has a renowned music school. Sports, athletic grounds, the Annual Bathtub Race and Rowing Club keep all youths in good form and have given Nanaimo the title of "Bathtub Racing Capital of the World".... Three newspapers, a radio station and a synchronized swimming team of ladies keep all abreast with the exciting daily news.

Culturally, the theatre, concerts and festivals by ethnic groups keep everybody happy and hotels, quality restaurants, pubs and inexpensive restaurants cater for entertain-ment. Recent development of high density housing is a good sign of growth.

Climate is mild in winter as well as summer (Jan, +15 to -17;   Jul, +2.8 +36)

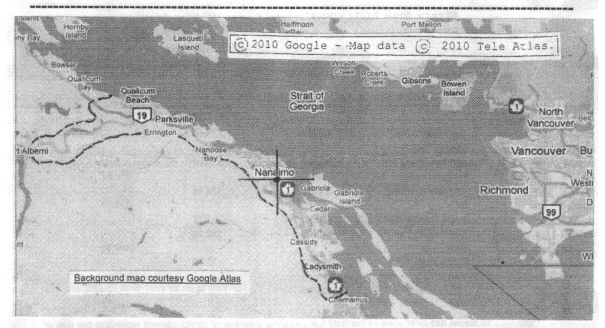

Background map courtesy Google Atlas

Nanaimo, Ladysmith, Nanoose Bay, Port Alberni.

Age Structure		Socio-economics		$ Incomes		Languages	
0-19	95%	Mang/Prof	88%	10k-29k	77%	English	51%
20-24	119%	Clerical w	96%	30k-49k	48%	French	10%
25-64	97%	Skilled w	113%	50k-79k	39%	Chinese	18%
65+	132%	Others	124%	80k +	3%	Other	21%

Founded as a trading post in 1849, after discovery and mining of coal, the "Nanaimo Bastion" started to export it. Next stage was to build a commercial fishing fleet, trade farm produce and saw lumber. An Oceanographic Research Station is now a main employer. Nanaimo is known as the "Hub city" (virtually at Vancouver Island's central city) colloquially, "Hub, Tub and Pub" city. It is frequently linked by ferry and hydroplane to Vancouver and Victoria. Median household income = $46,000 (BC = $52,709.

Vancouver Island University is centred in Nanaimo and has a renowned music school. Sports, athletic grounds, the Annual Bathtub Race and Rowing Club keep all youths in good form and have given Nanaimo the title of "Bathtub Racing Capital of the World".... Three newspapers, a radio station and a synchronized swimming team of ladies keep all abreast with the exciting daily news.

Culturally, the theatre, concerts and festivals by ethnic groups keep everybody happy and hotels, quality restaurants, pubs and inexpensive restaurants cater for entertainment. Recent development of high density housing is a good sign of growth.

Climate is mild in winter as well as summer (Jan, +15 to -17;   Jul, +2.8 +36)

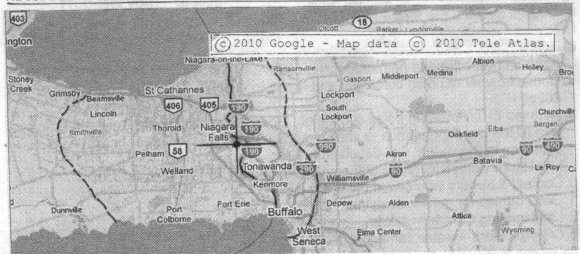

Niagara Falls-St. Catherine's, Beamsville, Lincoln, Smithville, Thorold, Fort Erie, Welland, Port Colborne, Niagara-on-the-Lake.

Age Structure		Socio-economics		$ Incomes		Languages	
0-19	120%	Mang/Prof	81%	10k-29k	56%	English	83%
20-24	107%	Clerical w	103%	30k-49k	110%	French	10%
25-64	98%	Skilled w	106%	50k-79k	31%	Chinese	5%
65+	89%	Others	116%	80k +	7%	Other	2%

Developing an economy based on wine-production and particularly tourism, this city region faces some competition from the US neighbours - Buffalo and Tonawanda - but their current decline due to the world economic recession, gives the better-faring Canadian side a better chance to grow. A great deal depends on developing more service and technological industries and the tolerance of municipalities to allow enterprise to devise innovations in tourist activity and specialized retail boutiques with items almost unheard of on the other side of the border. Positive business attitude and novelty will create initiatives to rival US competitors.

Niagara University helps in that direction by producing more graduates in computer science and information technology. Niagara College has a campus in Niagara-on-the-Lake and other training facilities for the new generation are fairly well distributed over the city region.

Cultural facilities are comparatively few:- Daredevil Gallery, Convention halls, Fort Erie Public Library, local history museums and some monuments to 1812 war heroes and the memorial at the Chippawa Battlefield Heritage Park. A remarkable restoration is the Niagara Apothecary featuring an 1866 pharmacy. St. Catherine's Museum At Lock 3 with a viewing platform to watch ships of 50 nations. The Ontario Federation of Indian Friendship Centres performs a social as well as cultural service, encouraging the cultivation of fruit and grapes.

Niagara Falls is a unique geographical phenomenon, attracting visitors from all over the world. Nearby luxury hotels, casinos, quality restaurants and night clubs produce a lively night atmosphere and quite a congestion of tourist coaches, cars and buses. But the natural falls produce a glorious waterfall noise that drowns all others. A shuttle service is operated to transfer tourists from USA to view the Falls and enjoy the cosmopolitan atmosphere for a few hours. Bus service joins all three towns and the Welland Canal now serves recreation as well as trade.

St. Catherine airport serves the entire city region and it is bound to grow. Exiting entertainment facilities include restaurants, luxury hotel lounges, pubs, etc.

Climate of the region is mild and very sunny, highly favourable to farming and cattle growing.

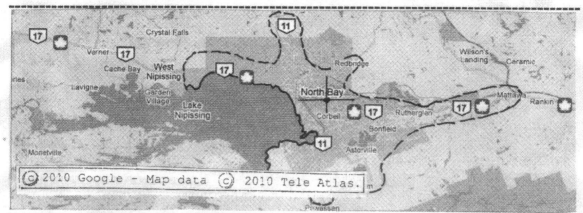

North Bay, Verner, Field, Sturgeon Falls, Kiosk, Mattawa, Rutherglen, Tomiko, Astorville, Bonfield, Corbeil, Redbridge, Chisholm.

Age Structure		Socio-economics		$ Incomes		Languages	
0-19	106%	Mang/Prof	105%	10k-29k	38%	English	79%
20-24	121%	Clerical w	115%	30k-49k	114%	French	15%
25-64	94%	Skilled w	117%	50k-79k	21%	Chinese	1%
65+	109%	Others	109%	80k +	6%	Other	5%

In 1851 she was a lumber town. Coal was later mined. Three rail lines and two hwys soon criss-crossed nearby. During the Cold War, a Royal Canadian Air Force base developed and a long runway was built for jets. Today, a large airport connects the city to most Canadian and US cities. Part of the site has become the Memorial Gdns Ice-Skating Rink and sites are serviced for light industry. Most progressive is the ratio of 23.5% production to 76.5% service, as shown by fibre optics being used for infrastr're + Internet services. Magazines have named North Bay as "No 1 in North Ontario", "One of the 20 greatest places to live" and studies have declared her 16th among 154 cities.

Nipissing University and Commanda College (Aviation, Commerce and Education dpts) have received accolades. Six institutions offer courses from hairstyling to languages.

The Capitol Centre Theatre (1,000 seats), Waterfront earmarked for an Entertainment Centre over and above the water sports, swimming and boating enjoyed at present plus Heritage Carousel, Rail Mini-train, Chief Commanda II play ship - all designed for child play - arouse no wonder where the Dionne Quints Museum was built to glorify their birth and the 3 million people that came to see them. The poor mother must have cursed ...

North Bay District Hospital and the Northeast Mental Health Centre cater for all health needs of a wide region, much more extensive than the city region on the above map.

There are 3- and 4-star hotels in addition to restaurants and pubs for entertainment. Low density housing, good urban services, moderate climate, fresh air, greenery and

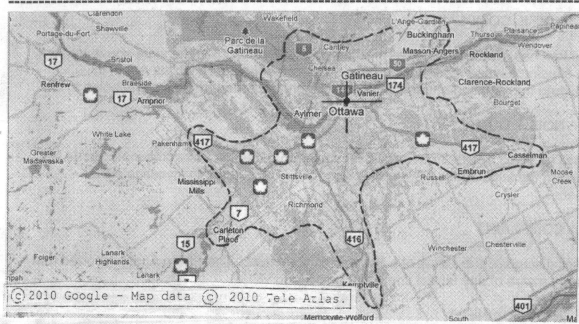

Ottawa, Nepean, Orleans, Carleton Place, Richmond, Kemptville, Embrun, Casselman,Vanier,
Aylmer, Pakenham, Mississipi Mills, Stittsville, Chelsea, Buckingham, L'Ange Gardien, Cantley,

Age Structure		Socio-economics		$ Incomes		Languages	
0-19	108%	Mang/Prof	141%	10k-29k	32%	English	29%
20-24	93%	Clerical w	112%	30k-49k	121%	French	27%
25-64	124%	Skilled w	87%	50k-79k	31%	Chinese	19%
65+	102%	Others	76%	80k +	12%	Other	25%

Fourth Metro area and a megalopolis in the making, Ottawa, amalgamated as a matter
of policy with Gatineau, will grow on both sides of the Ottawa river and along the 417
and 416 main roads, rather the Rideau Canal.The latter was built as a defensive measure by its founder Col. By, but is now a great recreational waterway. Service has been
the main industry in parallel with growth as the Federal capital and decision centre, and
as such, it was bound to attract info-technology. Norton and over a hundred computer
related companies made it the Silicon Valley of the North. Pharmaceuticals is another
growing modern industry and the few manufacturers produce no pollution. The growing
Ottawa Intern'l Airport serves Government, Universities, Tourism and office workers.

Two Universities - the bilingual Ottawa U and monolingual Carleton U - train some
34,000 students in Law, Informatics, Arts and Sciences. Associated cultural facilities
are the Arts Gallery, Observatory, Museums, the renovated Natural History Museum.

Entertainment facilities are few, with quality restaurants and Chateau Laurier hotel at
the highest level. There is also a TV studio and Radio station. Many ethnic communities
organize their festival, but the Tulip Festival and Winterfest are at the top.
The climate is "cool, continental, with warm summers and the occasional hot day."

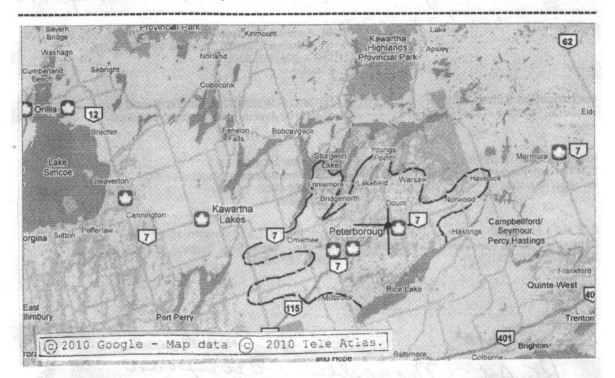

Peterborough, Omemee, Bridgenorth, Ennismore, Lakefield, Douro, Norwood, Warsaw .

Age Structure		Socio-economics		$ Incomes		Languages	
0-19	95%	Mang/Prof	97%	10k-29k	37%	English	87%
20-24	108%	Clerical w	108%	30k-49k	89%	French	9%
25-64	91%	Skilled w	102%	50k-79k	18%	Chinese	2%
65+	96%	Others	110%	80k +	5%	Other	2%

The city has a strong economy in the goods and services sector and forms a major transport stop on highway 7. It was the earliest city to start generating hydro-electricity. The 1904 Hydraulic Lift Lock is among the highest in the world. The city runs her own bus transit network, extending to many towns and villages in the region. Tourism and recreation related to the Trent-Severn Canal contribute significantly to the economy.

Trent University located in the city has a strong Environmental Studies Program and the climate of the region is already being considered as a major factor in the design of all public facilities including waste management. A positive factor is the harsh Canadian winter, which makes for high quality grain crops - one of the city regions products.

While physical recreation facilities cater adequately for the University studentship, higher levels of cultural and entertainment facilities are lacking. Entrepreneurs and municipalities in the city region, have therefore a challenge:- how to provide these higher level facilities which tourists and students are prepared to pay for and enjoy. Inns restaurants and pubs are to be seen in every town and village in the city region.

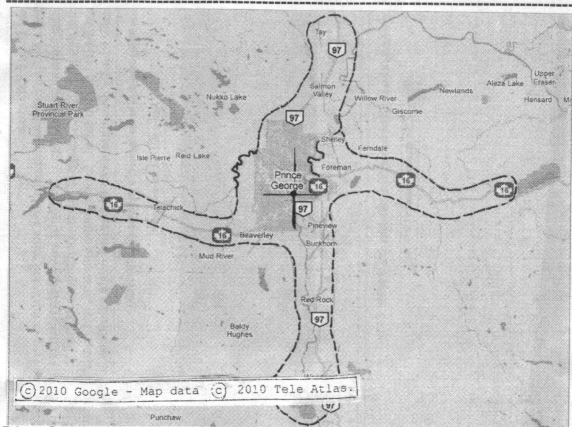

Prince George , Woodpecker, Red Rock, Beaverley, Telachick, Tay, Buckhorn, Pineview, Foreman, Shelley, Shelley, Salmon Valley.

Age Structure		Socio-economics		$ Incomes		Languages	
0-19	90%	Mang/Prof	99%	10k-29k	76%	English	79%
20-24	117%	Clerical w	111%	30k-49k	91%	French	6%
25-64	126%	Skilled w	110%	50k-79k	75%	Chinese	4%
65+	138%	Others	147%	80k +	7%	Other	13%

Originated as Fort George in 1807, which being built in timber, was the earliest use of a local resource to lead to an entire industry in the Province. That Fort has become the largest city in northern BC, but the need for major government-funded services to support the population's needs is still evident. The Columbia River project to generate electricity for BC Hydro was a great step forward for the city region's economy. A Chamber of Commerce provides guidance to entrepreneurs and developers as to best location and labour resources for their project. Local natural history, and the development of lumbering and transportation are illustrated in the Fort George Regional Museum, while Fort St. James in the city region shows Canada's largest collection of 19th century fur trade buildings still on their original sites. Higher education, cultural, entertainment, recreation and specialized shopping facilities would stimulate the economy as well as meeting social need in the entire north of BC..
The mild climate as regards winter snows and summer heat has led to a relaxed lifestyle.

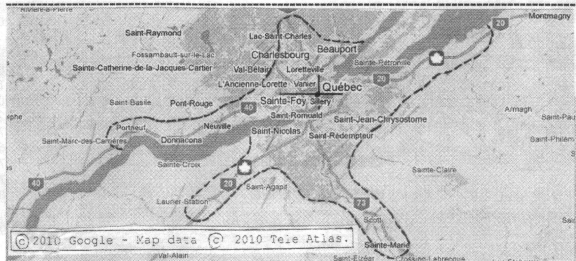

Ville de Quebec, Saint-Marc-des-Carrieres, Portneuf, Donnacona, Neuville, Scott, St. Nicholas, St. Redampteur, Ste Marie, St.- Jean-Chrysostome, St. Rumuald, Sillery, Ste-Foy, Val Belair, L'Ancienne Lorette, Vanier, Loretteville, Charlesbourg, Beauport, Lac St Charles.

Age Structure		Socio-economics		$ Incomes		Languages	
0-19	91%	Mang/Prof	138%	10k-29k	74%	English	5%
20-24	120%	Clerical w	130%	30k-49k	142%	French	78%
25-64	111%	Skilled w	104%	50k-79k	81%	Chinese	6%
65+	87%	Others	84%	80k +	14%	Other	11%

Quebec ("where the river narrows" in Algonquin) is a UNESCO World Heritage Site and unique walled city in America. The economy is lively, thanks to the location on the Toronto-Quebec grwth axis of Canada. Administrative functions, education (University of Quebec) culture and tourism are the main functions, with cultural and historic monuments holding the lasting impressions of tourists.

Base Ville and Haute Ville surround the Chateau Frontenac - a dominant landmark.. The star-shaped Haute Ville Citadelle. Notre Dame basilica, Notre Dame des Victoires, Musee de Quebec in Parc des Champs de Bataille (art collection and free concerts) and Musee de la Civilisation are among the exceptional cultural monuments of the city. The Literary and Historical Society is among top attractions.

The most extensive (sculpture, dog sled racing, snow-bathing) winter festival in the world; Horse drawn sleigh rides an International Canoe Race are dogsled races are other annual events. Famous are the Montmorrency Falls (272 ft high) Lively café culture and boutiques make for lively specialized shopping. The climate is humid continental, with sunny days in summer.

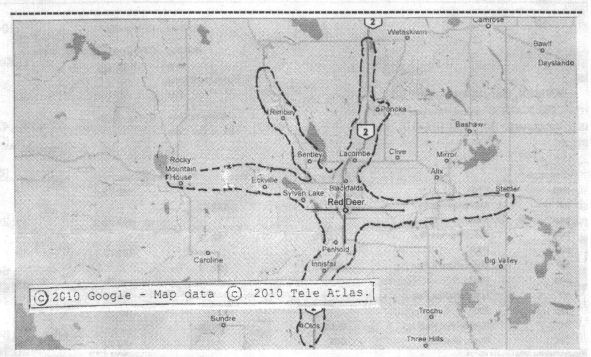

Red Deer, Benalto, Sylvan Lake, Blackfalds, Joffre, Penfold, Innisfail, Bowden.
Bentley, Leslieville, Clive, Penoka.

Age Structure		Socio-economics		$ Incomes		Languages	
0-19	107%	Mang/Prof	106%	10k-29k	37%	English	67%
20-24	94%	Clerical w	94%	30k-49k	114%	French	13%
25-64	109%	Skilled w	109%	50k-79k	21%	Chinese	6%
65+	82%	Others	113%	80k +	1%	Other	14%

A city region of major economic expansion, aiming to form a petroleum-based industrial
cluster. Manufactures and services are on a growing scale and it is only the location
between two major competitive centres that will delay - but not arrest - its growth.

It has - and in the course of growth - it will acquire educational, health and entertainment facilities.

Culturally well-worth visiting is the Royal Tyrrell Paleontolohy Museum, set in the heart
of the arid Red Deer Valley. An architecturally well-designed building, set where the
bones were found, but not near any other urban facilities, other than Damheller village.
Within the city region is also the Rocky Mountain House with two 1840 chimneys
nearby, remnants of old forts.   Nearer Red Deer is the Wetaskiwin Reynolds Museum
of antique vehicles and the Reynolds Alberta Museum, exhibiting the development of
agriculture, industry and transportation in Alberta.

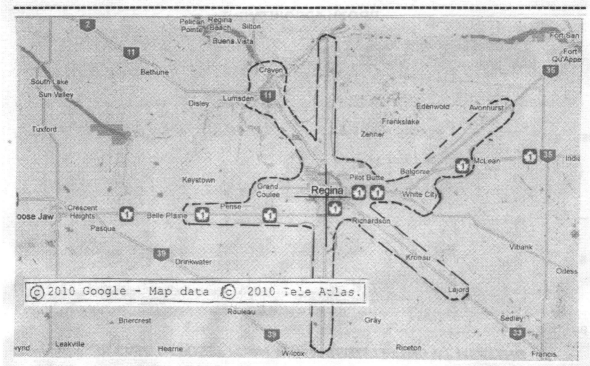

Belle Plaine, Pense, Grand Coulee, Craven, Lumsden, Pilot Bute, Balgonie, Avonhurst, McLean, White City, Lajord, Kronau, Richardson.

Age Structure		Socio-economics		$ Incomes		Languages	
0-19	89%	Mang/Prof	139%	10k-29k	29%	English	58%
20-24	94%	Clerical w	118%	30k-49k	102%	French	10%
25-64	121%	Skilled w	87%	50k-79k	14%	Chinese	9%
65+	87%	Others	73%	80k +	3%	Other	23%

Tourism in Saskatchewan has grown under Regina's Provincial initiative, building some 600 varied institutions - museums, galleries, theatres and archeological sites being developed over some 100 years. Bateman, Diefenbaker, Mendel Art , Outlook District and others - all have had a part to play in this long teleological planning tradition.
Four National and 37 Provincial parks are also administered from Regina offices run by professional and clerical workers, earning middle range and high salaries.

Regina's share of these institutions includes the RCMP Heritage Centre , Royal SK museum, Shumiak Art Gallery,   Ecological Museum of Canada,   RCMP Academy (Parade + Sunset retreat ceremonies), Saskatchewan Western Development Museum; Gull Lake Interpretative Centre and the Saskatchewan Railway Museum.

All this wealth in cultural and related institutions has also attracted an infrastructure of associated entertainment facilities - cafes, restaurants, bookstores, hotels, etc - and the number of ethnic communities has given rise to dozens of festivals and social events.

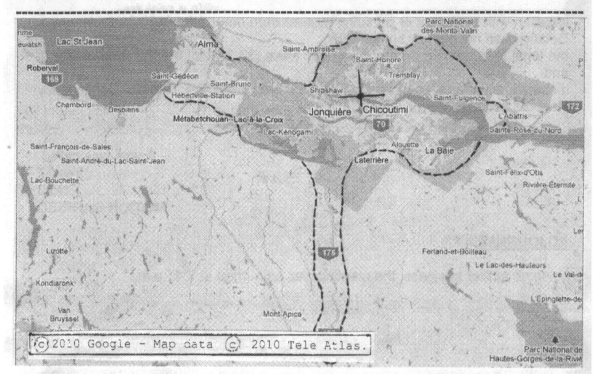

Chicoutimi, Jonquiere, Alma, St. Gedeon, St Bruno, Hebertville-Station, La Baie, Ste-Rose-du-Nord, L'Abattis, St. Fulgence, Alouette, Tremblay, St. Honore, St. Ambroise, Shipshaw, Laterriere, Lac Kenogami, Metabetchouan-Lac-a-la-Croix

Age Structure		Socio-economics		$ Incomes		Languages	
0-19	82%	Mang/Prof	81%	10k-29k	58%	English	5%
20-24	95%	Clerical w	104%	30k-49k	104%	French	83%
25-64	127%	Skilled w	103%	50k-79k	16%	Chinese	2%
65+	134%	Others	110%	80k +	3%	Other	10%

Hydro-Quebec's Peribonka development in the Saguenay-Lac-Saint-Jean region during 2004-8 procrued goods and services worth nearly 2.7billion in 2008.

Effects of the 1996 flood in the region and the 1998 ice storm in Montreal and Ottawa, led to cautionary measures being taken to foresee and forestall disasters due to storms and floods warned by Environment Canada's Meteorological Service.

The Government of Canada made a major investment by granting funds to a company wishing to produce a new animal feed and help create new markets beyond the Province.

At St. Felicien just east of the city region, there is a Zoological Parc with moose, birds and other animals roam free over 400 acres. Inside the city region there is Saguenay Park bisected by the river and containing a huge 1881 statue of Our Lady of the Saguenay. Where the river meets the St. Lawrence Seaway, Tadoussac and Chauvin's House mark the first trading post in Canada. The climate of Saguenay region is subpolar with long winters and short summers.

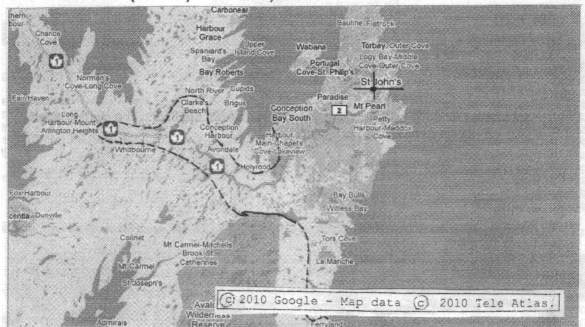

St. John's, Torbay, Outer Cove, Pouch Cove, Bauline, Flatrock, Wabana island, Mt. Pearl, Petty Harbour, Madox Cove, Paradise, Conception Bay South, Harbour, Main Chapel's Cove, Lakeview, Haywood, Avondale, Conception Harbour, Clarke's Beach, Harbour Mount, Arlington Heights, Whitbourne, Bay Bulls Wiless Bay, Tors Cove, La Manche, Cape Boyle, Calvert.

Age Structure		Socio-economics		$ Incomes		Languages	
0-19	89%	Mang/Prof	102%	10k-29k	27%	English	86%
20-24	96%	Clerical w	89%	30k-49k	185%	French	12%
25-64	109%	Skilled w	98%	50k-79k	37%	Chinese	1%
65+	123%	Others	132%	80k +	3%	Other	1%

Memorial University of St. John's & Corner Brook had a 2006 studentship of 18,172 - the largest in Atlantic Canada. Hibernia, White Rose, Terra Nova and Hebron oil fields gain 15% of GDP and are likely to give rise to a new technological university.   GDP of the Province was $31,277 billion, comparing favourably with other Canadian Provinces. Hotels and B&B accommodation are available in all coastal resorts. World Heritage Site of Gros Morne National Park, is noted for its unusual geological formation and fjords created by ice-age glaciers and tectonic movements.   Newfoundland's climate is "cool in summer" and "humid continental in winter", most enjoyable along the coast. The entire province is a tourist Paradise (name of a town in the hinterland).- as proved by ½ million tourists leaving $366 million in 2006.   The province's 7,000 year history will continue in greater prosperity thanks to increasing oil production and growing tourism.

Nevertheless, it takes 341 days waiting to see a psychiatrist and NFLD is getting old rapidly - after baby boom there was an abrupt fall in fertility rate. Health care in decline. Shortage of working age population, but incomes high due to oil production. Influx of immigrants is encouraged. St. John's population is growing but rural areas in decline. Investment in Education and Health in the coming decade is going to be crucial.

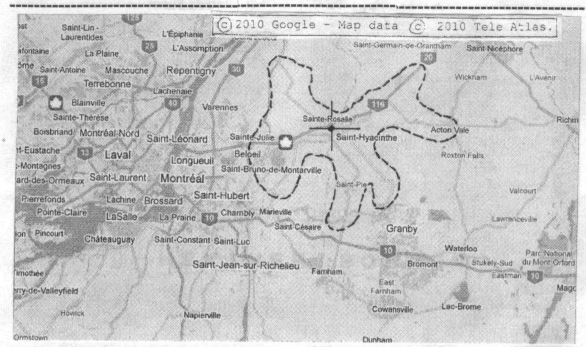

St. Hyacynthe, Saint-Rosalie, Acton Vale, Saint-Pie, St Bruno, Beloeil, Ste.Julie.

Age Structure		Socio-economics		$ Incomes		Languages	
0-19	110%	Mang/Prof	87%	10k-29k	37%	English	12%
20-24	97%	Clerical w	86%	30k-49k	98%	French	78%
25-64	121%	Skilled w	109%	50k-79k	8%	Chinese	3%
65+	103%	Others	97%	80k +	2%	Other	7%

The city's cross-roads location favoured her start as a rail station for loading and unloading goods under cover. Agriculture followed and today, the city boasts an agri-food science festival lasting 11 days. On a previous year, she also hosted an Internat'l Scientific Symposium and today, the city is a member of the Professional Development Institute of Tourism organization. Cultural facilities followed and a cultural diversity was generated with immigrants increasingly being involved.

Grants given as part of Canada's Economic Action Plan, new social housing units were built with schools and sports facilities. Establishment of a Wal-Mart store, boosted the economy. A 5-star hotel (l'Auberge des Seigneurs) followed.

Varied industries have developed over the decades and sports facilities were built in parallel. Research equipment will be housed in a recently built plant and the operation of cultural facilities will be improved

The climate is described as healthy. Moderate snow winters and cool summers.

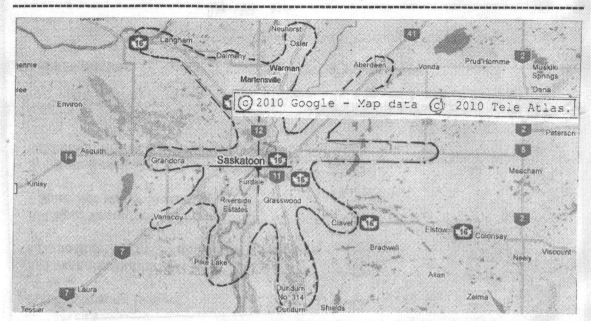

Saskatoon, Grandora, Langham, Dalmeny, Neuhorst, Osler, Warman, Martensville, Aberdeen, Clavet, Grasswood, Dunburn No 314, Pike Lake, Riverside Estates, Furdale, Vanscoy.

Age Structure		Socio-economics		$ Incomes		Languages	
0-19	96%	Mang/Prof	111%	10k-29k	43%	English	54%
20-24	113%	Clerical w	97%	30k-49k	103%	French	14%
25-64	116%	Skilled w	127%	50k-79k	23%	Chinese	9%
65+	126%	Others	135%	80k +	5%	Other	23%

Saskatoon is the largest potassium and uranium exporter in the world and the Province grows 45% of Canada's grain, exporting a good part of it through Vancouver. Oil and natural gas are becoming important, particularly when ethanol production is considered. The Western Economic Partnership Agreement established the Community Development Trust Fund, helping towns and villages develop. "The Saskatoon Star-Phoenix" has also reported that a similar fund had been established by the Saskatchewan Party.

Saskatchewan healthcare has been described as "socialized medicine" - doctors paid by the Province, not patients - according to need at any age

The city region's service Functions are shown in these 2006 employment statistics:-
Finance, Insurance, real estate: 17.1%   Education, health & social services: 11.9%

The highest production year was 1909 when many European immigrants were granted their own land, which they cultivated most enthusiastically.

Saskatoon's July temperatures vary between 11 and 25 degrees, while January temperatures vary between -12 and -22

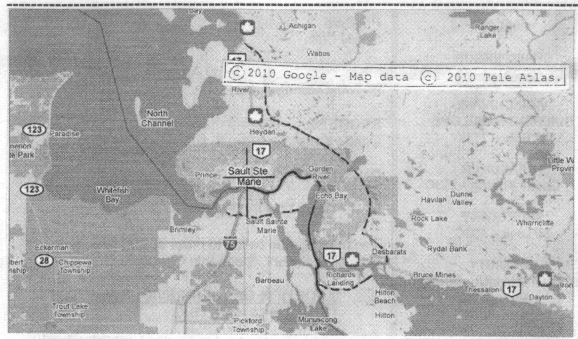

Prince, Goulais River,Heyden, Garden River, Echo Bay, Richards Landing, Desbarats,

Age Structure		Socio-economics		$ Incomes		Languages	
0-19	90%	Mang/Prof	85%	10k-29k	12%	English	52%
20-24	112%	Clerical w	97%	30k-49k	107%	French	25%
25-64	95%	Skilled w	113%	50k-79k	12%	Chinese	6%
65+	132%	Others	125%	80k +	3%	Other	17%

The city has an Economic Development Corporation to manage her economy and a significant success has been the stability of employment and increased activity of the airport, keeping the city region in touch with US and Canadian cities for transit services, lake shipping and tourism. The Corporation "is a leader in the provision of efficient, affordable and quality services to industry and population". In addition to steel production, recent action has been towards the modernization and diversification of industries, with information, technology and telecommuni-cation components. The arrival of new stores and entertainment facilities has been a stimulus to tourism, cultural (art gallery, museums), recreational and shopping facilities

A number of colleges relating to the city's industries and informatics operate and in 2011 there will be a convention of college representatives from all over Canada. A good number of cultural and entertainment facilities exist and the Cultural Board Community Recognition Awards are distributed each year. Lively team encounters take place in the John Rhodes Sports Stadium. The substantial percentage of French and Italian residents leads to many events and festivals being organized in the open air, as well as in restaurants, the cinema and sports venues.

The Algoma Health Unit provides hospital services to the entire city region.

The climate is humid continental due to lake currents, but summers are cool and pleasant.

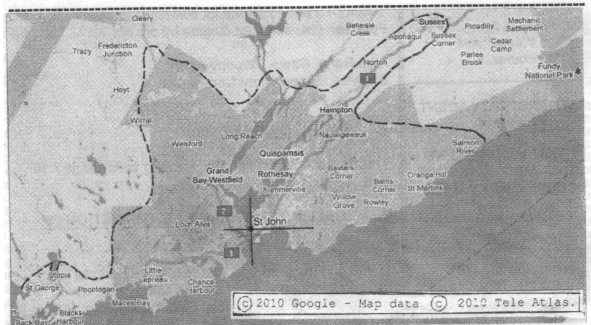

© 2010 Google - Map data © 2010 Tele Atlas.

St. John, Chance Harbour, Little Lepreau, Poologan, Blacks Harbour. St. George, Utopia, Black Bay, Wirral, Welsford, Grand Bay-Westfield, Long Reach, Quispammsis, Hampton, Rothesay, Summerville, Loch, Alva, Baxter's Corner, Neuwigeawauk, Salmon River, Orange Hill, St. Martins, Bains Corner, Willow Grove, Rowley, Norton, Apohaqui, Sussex Corner,

Age Structure		Socio-economics		$ Incomes		Languages	
0-19	82%	Mang/Prof	81%	10k-29k	58%	English	55%
20-24	95%	Clerical w	114%	30k-49k	104%	French	33%
25-64	127%	Skilled w	123%	50k-79k	36%	Chinese	2%
65+	134%	Others	110%	80k +	4%	Other	10%

St John has become a significant economic pole due to the production of electrical energy by the use of Bay of Fundy's pronounced tides. This will attract environmentally clean industries. The Provincial economy has traditionally been based on the exploitation of natural resources like forestry and fisheries, but technology is gaining momentum.   Urban areas gain services and keep employment high, but rural youth still migrate to central and western provinces for higher wages. Finance and Insurance are the economy's strongest sectors with tourism becoming increasingly more important and guidance on the web is helping . Addition of airports and extension of the bus transportation system to parks and villages   with optimal itineraries and automated heating and cooling encourages tourists to venture beyond the city.
"Royal St. John Gazette" was NB's first newspaper. NB University is based in Fredericton as well as St. John. Colleges offer short-term training courses in Info. Technology.   "Symphony New Brunswick" orchestra of St. John performs some 30 concerts a year.

Contrary to the humid continental temperate climate of northern NB,   St. John enjoys warmer winters and sunnier summers, allowing residents / visitors to enjoy the great outdoors green.
The climate is warmer inland than in coastal areas as it is continental rather than maritime
St. John is the foggiest port in the Province, but the problem is overcome with modern radar.

Sarnia, (part of Port Huron + Marysville), Plymouth, Petrolia, Wallaceburg

Age Structure		Socio-economics		$ Incomes		Languages	
0-19	120%	Mang/Prof	87%	10k-29k	47%	English	79%
20-24	97%	Clerical w	106%	30k-49k	108%	French	9%
25-64	131%	Skilled w	119%	50k-79k	28%	Chinese	5%
65+	96%	Others	97%	80k +	7%	Other	7%

A major community on the shores of Lake Huron and drawing some clientele for its first class medical facilities and services from Port Huron and Marysville in US A Physician Recruitment Taskforce has been set up to further this Function. Education, Social Science, Government Service and Religious higher education and training are some of the other functions carried out by Sarnia. The city has an oil refining and petrochemical production plant in Petrolia (see map). Canada "Jazz" airline provides a frequent service to Toronto. Still surviving is agriculture as a significant contributor to the economy.

Point Edward Charity Casino is part of a major entertainment complex with all facilities forming part of the Entertainment Function from drinking bar to Casino.

The City of Sarnia Information Center provides advice on establishing any new business, on media, utilities infrastructure, development permits, etc on friendly and easily accessible basis.

The climate is mild with a short winter season.

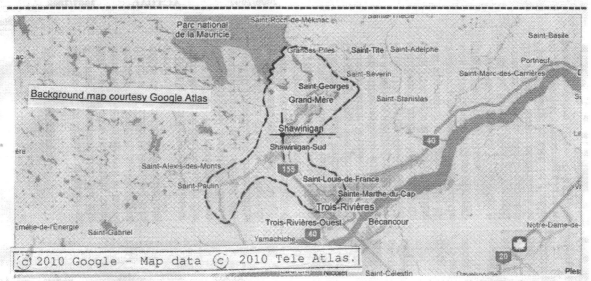

Background map courtesy Google Atlas

(c) 2010 Google - Map data (c) 2010 Tele Atlas.

Shawinigan, Grandes-Piles, Saint Georges, Shawinigan Sud, Saint-Louis de France, Grand-Maire, Saint-Paulin.

Age Structure		Socio-economics		$ Incomes		Languages	
0-19	89%	Mang/Prof	84%	10k-29k	61%	English	18%
20-24	114%	Clerical w	82%	30k-49k	84%	French	69%
25-64	118%	Skilled w	134%	50k-79k	9%	Chinese	3%
65+	112%	Others	143%	80k +	3%	Other	11%

Manufactures and services are present in this city region in great diversity and retired workers tend to stay and retire locally. Clinics and small hospitals take care of them. The presence of dense forests are considered as the pillar of the region's economy. They are the source of wood pulp and printing paper, which leads to service industries like writing and publishing. The proximity of Trois Rivieres and the Universite de Quebec of which a branch is located there, makes the establishment of a Shawinigan University less viable. The solution might be to establish a polytechnic and concentrate on informatics and computer manufacture and the leverage of the local MP could bring both

Shawinigan Falls is a tourist attraction by reason of the Falls and because Trois Rivieres is officially, the "National Poetry Capital of Quebec". An annual festival distributes prizes to new poets. On the city region's northern edge starts the magnificent wilderness of Parc National de la Mauricie with camping grounds, canoe and sailing lake, with an interpretive centre at Saint-Jean-des Piles. The Parc attracts a good number of visitors, local, national and even international. Entertainment facilities in it include bar, boutique, dining room, a meeting room and a picnic area. A guide for groups is sold at the interpretive centre.

The climate is partly cloudy but temperatures are between moderate and extreme.

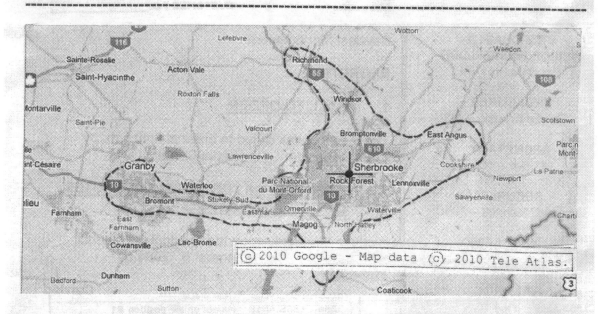

Granby, Rock Forest, Lennoxville, Cookshire, East Angus, Bromptonville, Windsor(Que) , Richmond, Mont Orford, Omerville, Eastman, Stukely-Sud, Waterloo, Bromont, Magog, North Hatley, Ayer's Cliff, Waterville., Granby (overlapping hinterlands)

Age Structure		Socio-economics		$ Income		Languages	
0-19	89%	Mang/Prof	84%	10k-29k	51%	English	18%
20-24	114%	Clerical w	92%	30k-49k	94%	French	69%
25-64	118%	Skilled w	124%	50k-79k	9%	Chinese	5%
65+	109%	Others	133%	80k +	3%	Other	8%

Sherbrooke gained from the influx of Empire Loyalists to south Quebec and still keeps a good 18% of Loyalist descendants, mostly bilingual and utterly faithful to their traditions. The 2009 recession left 13% vacancies and the City launched a survey to initiate a down- town development plan. Now, about 65 % of shoppers already approve the changes and no fewer than 6,000 shops operate profitably. There is adequate parking and good public transport, free to downtown workers and shoppers.   The 10-year development plan will culminate in a "Ville des Rivières" (Eastern Townships Regional Tourist Plan).

Sherbrooke University (with a branch in Montreal) and Sherbrooke students enjoy many cultural, sports and entertainment facilities, from art galleries and theatre to sing-songs in pubs. A large special library (dedicated to poetess Eva Sènècal) with tasteful murals is well used by all academics and proves a great resource. The Museum of Fine Arts, Dawn of Glass Art of Quebec, Eastern Townships Archives - all attract thousands of tourists.

Downtown specialized shops (from copper implements to videos) and services (finance to travel and insurance) include cinemas, bingo, night clubs and dance discotheques. In the city region there are also health clinics, retirement homes, and a re-training centre.

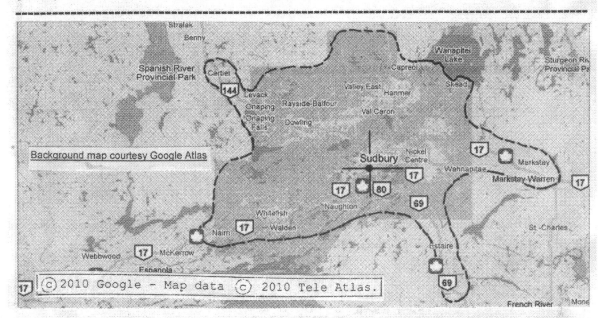

Background map courtesy Google Atlas

© 2010 Google - Map data © 2010 Tele Atlas.

Sudbury, Nickel Centre, Estaire, Wahnapitae, Markstay-Warren, Cartier, Naughton, Rayside-Balfour, Dawling, Levack, Onaping, Nairn, Onaping Falls, Whitefish, Walden, Markstay, Skead, Capreol, Hanmer, Val Caron, Valley East.

Age Structure		Socio-economics		$ Incomes		Languages	
0-19	89%	Mang/Prof	84%	10k-29k	61%	English	28%
20-24	114%	Clerical w	82%	30k-49k	94%	French	29%
25-64	138%	Skilled w	134%	50k-79k	9%	Chinese	12%
65+	82%	Others	143%	80k +	3%	Other	31%

Sudbury was the nickel mining city where the Canadian Mint established an entire industry in extracting the metal and minting coins, giving rise to two major tourist attractions .to the city - a huge nickel 10 cents coin and the less publicized piece of nickel mineral. The economy has followed the ups and downs of the world price of nickel, but many manufactures of household and steel items help to moderate the extremes. A booming economy when nickel's price on world markets was high, brought new manufactures and services. Major environmental improvements have resulted by increasing the height of industrial chimneys in order to send pollutants into the higher levels of the atmosphere. A Centre of Excellence in Mining Innovation was built. A regional airline offers a service to Toronto and this has increased tourism.

Health forms Sudbury's main Function. While mining remains a major influence on the region's economy, Sudbury's Cancer Centre has established her role as Health provider for the region

The region's population may be divided into three:- French, English and allophone, in roughly equal parts. Consequently, the education system is also divided into three.
Cultural events - festivals - are also initiated by these three population components.

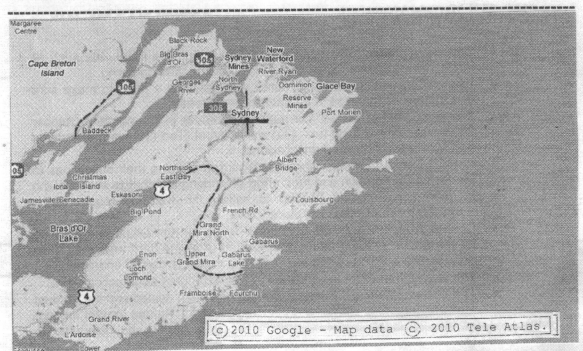

Sydney, Cabarus Lake, Upper Grand Mira, Cabarus, Grand Mira North, French Road, Albert Bridge, Louisbourg, Northside East Bay, Port Morlen, Reserve Mines, Dominion, River Ryan, Sydney Mines, North Sydney, George's River, Big Bras d'Or, Black Rock, Baddeck.

Age Structure		Socio-economics		$ Incomes		Languages	
0-19	94%	Mang/Prof	85%	10k-29k	147%	English	85%
20-24	105%	Clerical w	89%	30k-49k	87%	French	12%
25-64	89%	Skilled w	115%	50k-79k	51%	Chinese	1%
65+	114%	Others	117%	80k +	1%	Other	2%

Nova Scotia's tourism generates some 40,000 jobs and keeps the average income in the Province at $47,100.   The traditional occupations of fishing, forestry and agriculture are still plentiful, but tourism is advancing rapidly.

Sydney was founded in 1785 and after celebrating its 200th anniversary in 33 communities in Cape Breton and beyond - with music, dancing and story telling - established the Celtic Colours Festival for Oct. 8-16 each year. This had a $5.5 million impact on the city and the Province and "Centre 200" was soon founded as an exhibition, sports, convention, entertainment and concert space - not the earliest example of festivals being invented as a city-growth device. The Golf Festival is also an international occasion. Sidney's most famous festival however is the July 16 "Tall Ships Festival" attracting a tremendous crowd of visitors, volunteers and crews.   It is organized by the Waterfront Corp Ltd with deck receptions to innovative ships and year after year, the profits grow.

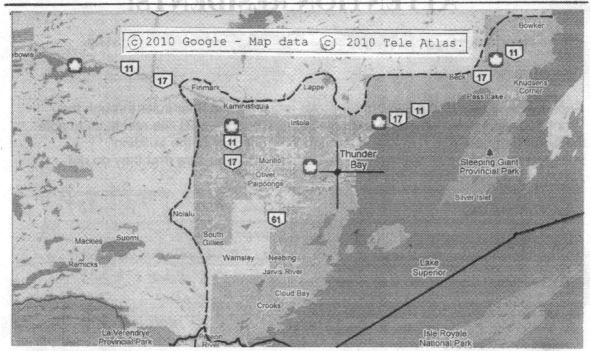

Thunder Bay, Knudsen's Corner, Bowker, Beck, Intola, Lappe, Kaministiqula, Murillo, Oliver Paipoonge, Cloud Bay, Crooks, Finmark, Nolalu, South Gilles, Wamsley, Neebin , Jarvis River, Pigeon River.

Age Structure		Socio-economics		$ Incomes		Languages	
0-19	87%	Mang/Prof	102%	10k-29k	21%	English	49%
20-24	91%	Clerical w	92%	30k-49k	89%	French	17%
25-64	119%	Skilled w	87%	50k-79k	9%	Chinese	9%
65+	141%	Others	143%	80k +	2%	Other	25%

Thunder Bay was formed in 1970 by the amalgamation of two cities through their urban renewal and the development of a climate-controlled shopping centre. One of the cities was Fort William (now a Historical Park and main tourist attraction) which had a concentration of Italians and Ukrainians, while Finmark neighbourhood had many immigrants from Finland.

Education and health services provide diversity from the forestry and manufacturing base of the city region. The Thunder Bay Regional Health Sciences centre and the creation of the Centre for Research and Innovation in Bio-sciences give a major Health Function which greatly extends the market of the city. Thunder Bay is now drawing visitors from Wisconcin, Minnesota & Michigan.
Cultural and entertainment events are much influenced by the high percentage of immigrant ethnic groups, forming some 25% of the population.

Passenger rail service to Thunder Bay ended in January 1990 and now, coach services stopping at Thunder Bay, service regional and national destinations.

The climate is influenced by Lake Superior and summers are cool, winters warm.

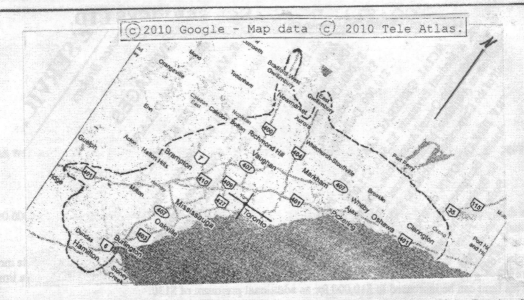

Toronto Centre, York, Mississauga, Oakville, Burlington, Stony Creek, Hamilton, Ajax, Dundas, Milton, Hornby, Halton Hills, Brampton, Vaughan, Markham, Whitchurch-Stouffville, Aurora, East Gwillimbury, Bradford West, East Gwillimbury, Orona, Pickering, Clarrington, Oshawa, Whitby, Brooklin, Nobleton.

Age Structure		Socio-economics		$ Incomes		Languages	
0-19	113%	Mang/Prof	138%	10k-29k	78%	English	51%
20-24	125%	Clerical w	120%	30k-49k	141%	French	16%
25-64	100%	Skilled w	69%	50k-79k	152%	Chinese	21%
65+	72%	Others	118%	80k +	45%	Other	12%

Highest financial and business Canadian center where technology is the driving force. Dynamic activity center of the Golden Horseshoe and Canadian growth axis stretching to Quebec City. It has many skyscrapers. A truly cosmopolitan megalopolis, it is serviced efficiently by Pearson International and Billy Bishop airports. Administrative function in Queen's Park is the Provincial parliament with all linked facilities within a brief walk, as in the case of Toronto Stock Exchange. Tourism, Finance, Insurance, Investment, Entertainment, Culture, Metro city services are the major functions, but it is also a major center for gay and lesbian 'culture' with quality restaurants pubs and Greektown restaurants for gourmets..

Ethnically, the most diverse city (UNESCO) reverted to its native name ('meeting place") in 1834 attracting new immigrants. There appears to be no limit to the growth of this megalopolis. Traffic flows fairly smoothly because major freeways slice the urban mass and the grid between them provides alternatives to a destination. Fast train and bus public transport (third largest in the continent) work efficiently and only Yorkville, Kensington Market and Eaton center may be called 'congested'. Other shopping in chic boutiques is specialized on fashion wear, jewelry and shoes The Blue Jays and three other teams have the Skydome and all other required sport facilities at hand and the Canada and the Golf Halls of Fame are the pinnacles ("Bata Shoe Museum") Global TV and Radio provide good Canada-wide entertainment and film production is also lively. Two symphony orchestras and some 50 dance companies, orchestras, dozens of music venues and theatres. Festivals include the Caribana, Pride Week, National Exhibition and Intern'l Film. The CN Tower (until 1908, tallest in the world) , Mc Michael Art Gallery, St. Michael Cathedral, War Museum, Canada's Wonderland, Ontario Science Center, Royal Botanical Gardens, Zoo, Wild Water Kingdom, Gardiner Museum of Ceramic Art, heritage sites, wooded ravine theme parks (Don Valley Brick Works), the Toronto Islands, etc - they all attract millions of tourists.

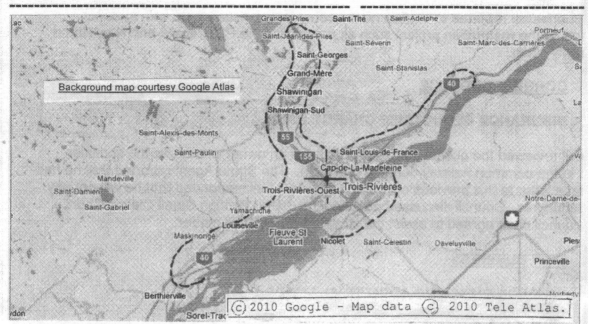

Trois Rivieres centre, Cap-de-la-Madeleine, St.Louis-de-France, Trois Rivieres Ouest, Shawinigan, Shawinigan-Sud, Grand-Mere, St.Georges, Nicolet, St-Jean-des-Piles, Maskinonge, Louisville, Yamachiche.

Age Structure		Socio-economics		$ Incomes		Languages	
0-19	76%	Mang/Prof	90%	10k-29k	44%	English	6%
20-24	90%	Clerical w	96%	30k-49k	96%	French	86%
25-64	121%	Skilled w	117%	50k-79k	11%	Chinese	3%
65+	122%	Others	109%	80k +	7%	Other	5%

This is a city region of a number of sizable towns, which, given favourable economic conditions will coalesce into a megalopolis thanks to the location in the middle between Montreal and Quebec city. It was Canada's 2nd city, having been founded in 1634 by the Sulpician and Jesuit clerics. Some manufactures date from that early date, having survived the great 1908 fire.

Part of the University of Quebec is located at Trois Rivieres.

Cultural facilities:- Ursulines Museum (1697), Manoir Boucher-de-Niverville, Tonnancour Manoir, Maison Hertel-de-la-Fresniere and the Trois Rivieres and Madeleine cathedrals The latter has an entire park decorated with sculptures of saints.

On the city region's northern edge starts the magnificent wilderness of Parc National de la Mauricie with camping grounds, canoe and sailing lake, with an interpretive centre at Saint-Jean-des Piles.

The port of Trois Rivieres has an occasional upsurge for jobs   for which there is a need in the region.

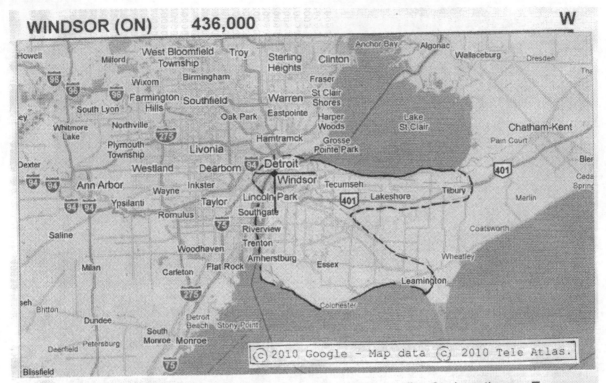

Windsor (ON), Belle River, Tilbury, Leamington, Kingsville, Amherstburg, Essex. Small part of Detroit - a megalopolis in decline - is assumed to be part of Windsor's hinterland

Age Structure		Socio-economics		$ Incomes		Languages	
0-19	102%	Mang/Prof	97%	10k-29k	43%	English	73%
20-24	98%	Clerical w	116%	30k-49k	123%	French	7%
25-64	86%	Skilled w	89%	50k-79k	22%	Chinese	11%
65+	90%	Others	99%	80k +	9%	Other	8%

Windsor International Airport has many scheduled flights to US cities and also receives a good number from Canadian ones. Important sources of income are also educational services and car parts manufacture.
As the last Canadian city on the growth axis to Quebec city and the first along the transport routes to the Great Lakes giant industrial complex, it only stands to gain from any trade increase between US and Canada.

Noteworthy cultural facilities are:- The Art Gallery (19th and 20th century artists of local history) the Francois Baby House (18th to 21st century changing exhibits of domestic life and implements) the Coventry Gardens and Peace Fountain rising 75 ft high and featuring special light effects, the Willistead Manor 36 room Tudor style mansion with carved wood paneling and Carrara marble fireplaces, on 15 acres of green landscape.

The climate is humid continental climate with warm days throughout the summer verging to hot.

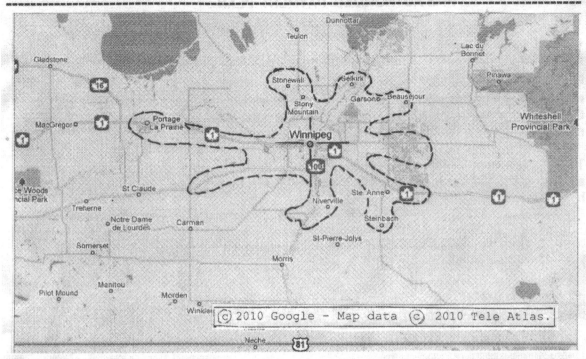

Winnipeg, Portage La Prairie, Stonewall Selkirk, Beausejour, Lewis, Seine, Richer, Steinbach, La Salle, Elm Creek

Age Structure		Socio-economics		$ Incomes		Languages	
0-19	91%	Mang/Prof	129%	10k-29k	30%	English	49%
20-24	96%	Clerical w	118%	30k-49k	105%	French	29%
25-64	120%	Skilled w	90%	50k-79k	15%	Chinese	2%
65+	138%	Others	97%	80k +	4%	Other	20%

Located in the middle of a vast country, this city has grown rapidly to become an important node in road, rail, aviation, TV and radio and tele-communication links with every major city in Canada and the US. She is a vast warehouse for transit goods waiting for transportation inland or abroad. In addition, a richly diverse industry has grown and it is up to her city planners to form technological, service and industrial complexes that will develop close linkages towards more innovation and profit.

The University is at the top of the Education Function and there are a few schools and colleges on subjects related to the city's functions. Winnipeg Art Gallery and other cultural facilities call for associated recreational and entertainment facilities, besides the luxury and other hotels catering for transportation needs.

Winnipeg has the lowest electricity charges because of the abundance of running waters. - often causing floods. The city region has a rich ethno-cultural mix.

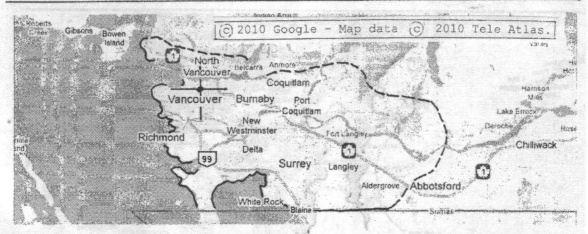

Vancouver City, Burnaby, New Westminster, Delta, Surrey, White Rock, West Vanc'ver
Delta, Richmond, Port Coquitlam, Fort Landley, Langley, Aldersgrove, North Vanc'ver,.

Age Structure		Socio-economics		$ Incomes		Languages	
0-19	94%	Mang/Prof	143%	10k-29k	87%	English	49%
20-24	121%	Clerical w	119%	30k-49k	137%	French	9%
25-64	89%	Skilled w	138%	50k-79k	149%	Chinese	31%
65+	147%	Others	90%	80k +	21%	Other	11%

Service-based economy - retirement, education, entertainment, specialized shopping and info-
tech. Sheltered deep harbour and coal mining made it ideal for exports to Pacific ports. Seabus,
Skytrain and Translink network make all parts accessible within 30mins. despite high residential
density (5,000 p / sq. km).   This, among other factors, made Vancouver Canada's fastest
growing Metro city in 2010 and a tourist heaven during the Winter Olympics.

Education outlets include five universities and many colleges catering from computation to
fashion design and cosmetics technology.   Near the universities are many sports and athletic
facilities - Canucks club, etc. There are also many ethnic institutions to satisfy the educational,
cultural, linguistic and traditional ethnic dance festival needs.

The Art Gallery has been collecting paintings of local (Emily Carr) and European artists and
holds 2-3 special exhibitions per annum. Vancouver Arts Club and 10 theatre venues present
classical, comedy or literary plays. Several museums, Central Library, Memorial and many
branch libraries, Van Dusen Botanical gardens, Gastown Clock and aboriginal art galleries,
monuments to city founders, Sun Yat Sen (Chinese) gardens are all a delightful escape from
congestion. Granville Island is a remarkable gain from a former industrial unsightly collection of
buildings. Whale watching, white water rafting, Festival of Light, Lookout Rotating Restaurant
and modern watercraft will interest many visitors in a fully cosmopolitan, easy-going lifestyle.
There are seven large shopping centres catering for diverse specialist tastes on jewelry, shoes,
clothing, groceries, animal lovers and even sports bikes. Retail pharmacies cater for the needs
of the retired and dozens of retirement homes suit any pocket.

Investment seminars train people to use VSE - the third largest stock exchange after Toronto
and Montreal.   It specializes in bullion, currency and jewelry.

VICTORIA (BC)   248,000

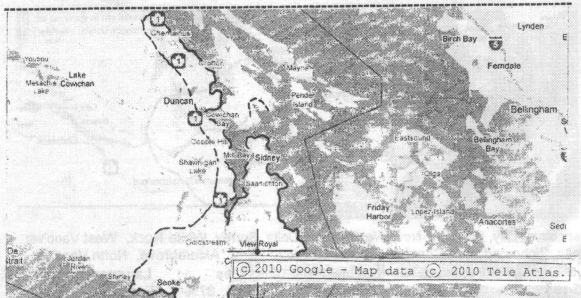

Victoria, View Royal, Colwood, Metchosin, Sooke, Goldstream, Cowichen Bay, Crofton, Chemainus, Oak Bay.

Age Structure		Socio-economics		$ Incomes		Languages	
0-19	90%	Mang/Prof	122%	10k-29k	76%	English	68%
20-24	113%	Clerical w	119%	30k-49k	127%	French	10%
25-64	126%	Skilled w	83%	50k-79k	138%	Chinese	9%
65+	137%	Others	117%	80k +	35%	Other	13%

Earliest growth was due to gold found in North Canada being sold in the city in 1858 "and the town was changed for ever".   The next economic prime mover was the Canadian Pacific reaching the West Coast.

Abundance of greenery among mostly Edwardian architecture. Butchart Gardens and the University located north of the city, keep it congestion free and her gradual expansion will eventually cover all of Saanich peninsula. Cultural facilities are also the Astrophysical Observatory, the Planetarium, the Butterfly Gardens, Christchurch Cathedral, Royal BC Museum, the ...Bug Zoo, Pacific Undersea Gardens, Art Gallery of Greater Victoria   and the Maritime and military museum of CFB Esquimault.   First Nations are remembered with traditional cabins and totem poles in beautifully landscaped Thunderbird Park. 1855 Craigflower School is the oldest in Western Canada.   Helmcken House (1852)

The climate is wet in winter and dry in summer (driest among Canadian cities).

It has some port functions, but they are tertiary to Administration and Culture and fully contributory to Tourism. City and port views of water greatly enhance tourism.

facilities are not to be seen, because the catchment is insufficient for them.

Canadian consumer USE FACTOR and facility LINKAGE values for Service Social Infractructure , (F) and PCP calculations
The following four tables show the proxy correlation values between:-
Demographic groups and facilities;   Facilities and geographical features

	Clinic	Rtmt	Welf	Phar	Dent	Doct	Dayc	Conc	Thetr	Galry	Musm	Cult	Liby	Com
Age0/19	.81	–	.71	.88	.86	.87	.88	.31	.37	.68	.52	.76	.73	.72
20/24	.63	–	.61	.72	.74	.75	–	.68	.72	.65	.84	.81	.84	.81
25/64	.57	–	.72	.78	.81	.80	–	.71	.74	.72	.78	.76	.68	.86
65+	.78	.89	.77	.82	.82	.83	–	.71	.76	.78	.66	.68	.70	.88
S/eM/P	.63	.74	.70	.71	.78	.82	.45	.81	.72	.77	.76	.81	.65	.81
Clerwk	.70	.61	.66	.67	.72	.78	.47	.69	.70	.72	.74	.77	.70	.84
Skilwk	.66	.64	.62	.71	.73	.79	.48	.52	.61	.68	.69	.52	.64	.78
Indfwk	.61	.54	.58	.70	.72	.81	.51	.49	.50	.51	.54	.46	.51	.69
$10-29	.81	.45	.31	.68	.71	.75	.53	–	.54	.46	.48	.52	.56	.59
$30-49	.79	.51	.44	.71	.75	.72	.63	.31	.62	.71	.61	.65	.61	.62
$50-79	.72	.46	.56	.74	.76	.75	.60	.63	.75	.74	.66	.76	.71	.70
$80+	.64	.42	.63	.76	.78	.81	.72	.71	.72	.77	.81	.71	.83	.72 .69
Anglo	.73	.56	.67	.70	.71	.72	.69	.74	.72	.71	.69	.73	.74	.73 75
Frnco	.81	.61	.72	.73	.74	.75	.71	.76	.74	.75	.72	.75	.74	.75 71
Orient	.82	.69	.61	.74	.75	.72	.73	.72	.61	.66	.70	.71	.75	.71
Other	.65	.71	.59	.62	.68	.69	.71	.65	.59	.61	.68	.74	.76	.69

	Clinic	Rtmt	Welf	Phar	Dent	Doct	Dayc	Conc	Thetr	Galry	Musm	Cult	Liby	Com
Sears	–	.76	.69	.85	–	–	–	–	–	–	–	–	–	.32
Bay	--	.78	.69	.85	–	–	–	–	–	–	–	–	–	.40
A&N	–	.79	.70	–	–	–	–	–	–	–	–	–	–	.39
Walm	.38	.86	.75	.86	–	–	–	–	–	–	–	–	–	.41
Zellr	.39	.87	.71	.65	–	–	–	–	–	--	–	–	–	.39
Jwel	–	.78	.67	–	–	–	–	–	–	–	–	–	–	.34
Comp	–	.56	.45	–	–	–	–	–	–	–	–	–	–	.47
Movr	–	.47	–	–	–	–	–	–	–	–	.35	–	.54	.45
Flwr	–	.76	.56	–	–	–	–	.71	.68	--	--	.56	--	.66
Moun	.68	.83	–	–	–	.68	–	–	–	–	–	–	–	--
Clim-														
Sun+	.34	.69	.34	.33	.56	.57	.69	–	–	–	–	–	–	.35
Mist	–	–	–	–	–	–	–	–	–	–	–	–	–	--
Hars	–	–	–	–	–	–	–	–	–	–	–	–	–	--

CODE   (Abbreviations)

Rtmt = Retirement home   **Welf** = Welfare society   **Pharm** = Pharmacy
Dent = Dentist   **Doct** = Family doctor   **Dayc** = Day care   **Conc** = Concert Hl
Thetr = Theatre   **Galry** = Art gallery   **Musm** = Museum   **Cult** = Cultural society
Liby = Branch library   **Com** = Community centre   **A&N** = Army & Navy store
WalM = WalMart store   **Zellr** = Zellers store   **Movr** = Home mover
Comp = Computer store   **Bldg** = Building materials store **Mist** = Mist / Pollution
Moun = Mountain resort site **Clim-** = Unfavourable climate **Hars** = Harsh weather

	Zoo	Glde	Stad	Sport	Swim	Golf	Bowl	Recs	Sailg	Camp	Hoky	Foot	Tenis	Park
Age0/19	.91	–	.79	.74	.86	–	.69	.54	.75	.84	.89	.94	.76	.96
20/24	.85	.84	.91	.95	.76	.73	.76	.85	.73	.86	.77	.79	.87	.91
25/64	.67	.86	.78	.87	.71	.78	.68	.74	.85	.89	.85	.72	.73	.86
65+	.36	–	–	.45	.32	.65	.78	.67	.65	–	.46	–	.43	.92
S/e M/P	.72	.86	.73	.68	.43	.56	.71	.52	–	.35	.51	–	.69	.83
Clerwk	.75	.72	.67	.72	.71	.70	.68	.66	.73	.56	.67	.64	.72	.79
Skilwk	.73	.81	.76	.79	.74	.84	.75	.67	.75	.67	.75	.67	.75	.72
Indfwk	.68	.54	.58	.77	.68	.66	.71	.63	.74	.77	.81	.77	.65	.76
$10-29	.74	–	.68	.67	.71	–	.69	.56	.67	.59	.86	.79	.59	.82
$30-49	.78	.53	.74	.72	.69	.54	.73	.64	.68	.65	.75	.76	.69	84
$50-79	.82	.67	.65	.70	.72	.69	.72	.72	.76	.56	.76	.67	.73	.78
$80+	.84	.78	.72	.68	.69	.78	.69	.73	.79	.53	.74	.65	.76	.72
Anglo	.85	.76	.70	.73	.71	.76	.70	.69	.78	.69	.75	.67	.78	.75
Frnco	.72	.59	.68	.72	.68	.59	.68	.56	.64	.70	.74	.69	.67	.77

CODE   (Abbreviations)
S/eM/P = socio-economic groups: Manager/Professionals **Other** = Allophones
Clerwk = Clerical workers **Skilwk** = Skilled workers   **Hoky** = Hockey arena
Indfwk = Indefinite workers   **$10-29** = $10,000-29,000 income group
Anglo = English speaking **Frnco** = French speaking+Acadian+Metis
Glde = Gliding club **Recs** = Recreational society   **Camp** = Camping ground